Evangelicals ON Public Policy Issues

Sustaining a Respectful Political Conversation

HAROLD HEIE

Contributors

Amy E. Black, Paul Brink, David P. Gushee,

Lisa Sharon Harper, Stephen V. Monsma, and Eric Teetsel

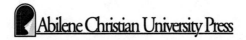

Abilene Christian University Press

EVANGELICALS ON PUBLIC POLICY ISSUES
Sustaining a Respectful Political Conversation

Copyright 2014 by Harold Heie

ISBN 978-0-89112-467-2
LCCN 2013026786

Printed in the United States of America

Scripture quotations, unless otherwise noted, are from The Holy Bible, New International Version. Copyright 1984, International Bible Society. Used by permission of Zondervan Publishers.

LIBRARY OF CONGRESS CATALOGING-IN-PUBLICATION DATA
Heie, Harold, 1935-
  Evangelicals on public policy issues : sustaining a respectful political conversation / Harold Heie.
      pages cm
  ISBN 978-0-89112-467-2
  1. Christianity and politics--United States. 2. United States--Social policy. 3. United States--Economic policy. 4. United States--Politics and government. I. Title.
    BR115.P7H436 2013
    261.70973--dc23

                                                                                    2013026786

Cover design by Jennette Munger
Interior text design by Sandy Armstrong, Strong Design

For information contact:
Abilene Christian University Press
1626 Campus Court
Abilene, Texas 79601

1-877-816-4455 toll free
www.abilenechristianuniversitypress.com

14 15 16 17 18 19 / 7 6 5 4 3 2 1

Evangelicals ON Public Policy Issues

Dedicated to Jim Skillen,
friend and mentor who
models respectful conversation

Contents

Public Policy Issues

Contributor Reflections

Foreword

Richard J. Mouw

When I was growing up in the evangelical world, respectful conversations among ourselves about issues of public policy was not a big problem that needed to be addressed, for two reasons. One was that we simply did not talk much about public policy questions, so there weren't many opportunities to show each other disrespect on this score. We saw ourselves as being on the margins of the larger culture in North America, a situation where we were convinced that our main obligation as evangelicals was one of getting people ready for heaven. Paying too much attention to major issues of public policy was viewed as bordering on a God-dishonoring "worldliness."

The second reason we did not argue with each other about public policy was that, when we did talk to each other about those matters, we pretty much agreed with each other. Our kind of people voted in elections mainly because we saw doing so as our civil duty, and when we did so, we took it for granted that we should cast our votes for conservative Republicans. To be sure, we knew how to be disrespectful with each other about things—modes of baptism, free will versus predestination, and different views of the millennium. But these were not the kinds of topics we thought about in the voting booth!

In recent years, though, intra-evangelical disrespect focusing on social-political-economic matters has become a visible reality. The change began to happen in the late 1960s, when some younger evangelicals who were concerned about civil rights and the Vietnam war openly contended with their elders about what they saw as the older generation's too-passive acceptance of the status quo. Soon that manifestation of "evangelical social action" came to be accompanied by other brands of activism, especially with the emergence of the Moral Majority in the 1980s.

Nor was the disrespectful tone an invention of the "religious Right," as is alleged in the commonly accepted version of the story. The disrespectful tone of voice about public policy can be heard across the evangelical spectrum. One of the traits that often unites evangelicals of differing perspectives is a gift for rhetorical overkill!

All of that is to say that this book is a fine gift to all of us. For evangelicals, it is a marvelous example of what it means to model civility to fellow evangelicals with whom we significantly disagree on controversial topics. And to the larger world, both Christians and non-Christians, it provides compelling evidence that evangelicals can indeed be gracious to one another, even when engaging in arguments about matters of serious concern that often generate considerable passion.

Our gratitude for this book extends also to the person who put it together. Harold Heie, one of our most talented conveners of respectful conversation, has himself been a model of the evangelical civility that he puts on display in the interaction among diverse viewpoints in these pages. This book, though, is not only a marvelous "how to" primer for engaging in respectful arguments. It is also an excellent "what" presentation, exploring the substance of urgent issues of concern for all who care about the common good.

An Alternative Political Conversation

The Brokenness of Political Discourse

This book is a second-stage follow-up to a completed electronic "Alternative Political Conversation." It all started as a result of my utter dismay at the pathetic state of contemporary political discourse. Three problems are obvious to even the most casual observer.

Vitriolic Political Conversation

It is painful to listen to politicians talking to, or about one another. Personal attacks are rampant. Too many political opponents revel in demonizing one another and impugning each other's motives. They often listen only to an echo of themselves, holding to fixed positions with little openness to learning from those with whom they disagree.

Unwillingness to Search for Common Ground

When political discourse deteriorates into advocating for unyielding fixed positions, there is little hope for finding the common ground that is needed for governing (rather than just getting elected). Seldom do we hear politicians on opposite sides of the aisle ask, "What can we agree on?"

Lack of Sustained Conversations about Disagreements that Could Lead to Sufficient Common Ground to Enable Legislation

Even if those on opposite sides of a given public policy issue are willing to acknowledge that an initial conversation uncovered some common ground, that rare accomplishment is typically not sufficient to inform possible legislation because of remaining significant disagreements. The only way to overcome this problem is if the parties are willing, after an initial conversation, to summarize those areas where agreement has been reached, identify the remaining disagreements, and commit to further conversations about differences, moving toward the goal of eventually identifying enough common ground to enable legislation.

There is a fourth major problem with current political discourse for those of us who profess to be "evangelical Christians."

Media Distortion of the Political Views of Evangelicals

The media typically portrays evangelicals as having a monolithic position on any given public policy issue, which is often an extreme position (generally on the "far right" end of the political spectrum). Such portrayals are often supported when media outlets interview only those evangelical spokespersons likely to hold extreme views, ignoring the many evangelicals who do not embrace such extremes. And the evangelicals they interview are also prone to advocating fixed positions, often resorting to vitriolic language and giving little evidence of respect for those with whom they disagree or of wanting to seek any common ground.

Modeling a Better Way

In order to begin addressing these four interrelated problems, I began the first stage of this project by hosting an electronic conversation (eCircle) on my website, www.respectfulconversation.net. Titled "Alternative Political Conversation" (APC), this conversation ran from February 1 through October 31, 2012. Its purpose was to *model respectful conversation between evangelical Christians who disagree about important public policy issues.*

With the help of Stephen Monsma, a senior research fellow at the Henry Institute for the Study of Christianity and Politics at Calvin College, I identified six scholars/practitioners in the realm of politics (including Monsma) who situated themselves at various points all along the political spectrum (from "left" to "right") and agreed to post position papers on preannounced public policy topics every three weeks for the nine-month duration of the electronic conversation.

I asked these six contributors to limit their initial postings on a given issue to 800–1,000 words. Given the complexity of the public policy issues they addressed, this severe word count limitation made it impossible for the contributors to say everything they may have wanted to say about any given issue. But the intended purpose of these initial postings was to get the conversation started.

Prior to the beginning of this electronic conversation, all of the six contributors indicated that they shared the common ground defined by the following "Basic Christian Principles for Politics and Public Policy."

1. **Truth-telling is essential.** Truth is often sacrificed by persons, political parties, and interest groups as they struggle to win elections and to sway public policies being adopted. But this is not the biblical way. Christians engaged in political discussions and debates ought always to tell the truth and to evaluate contending political forces by their truthfulness. This truth-telling includes avoiding not only

outright lies and fabrications, but also the telling of partial truths in an attempt to misrepresent or distort. (See Exod. 20:16.)

2.   All human beings are created by God and in his image. Men and women were created as God's image bearers and the crowning achievement of his creation. This means that all human beings possess an inherent, God-given worth or dignity that sets them apart from the rest of God's creation, and that all human beings, no matter what their gender, race, religion, ethnicity, or nationality have an inherent, equally great worth or dignity. (See Gen. 1:26–27.)

3.   Human beings are both fallen and capable of redemption. The human heart is inclined towards selfishness and evil, but through God's loving work, redemption and human progress—while limited—is possible. Although governments and their public policies can bring about good in society, they will always be subject to flaws and failures. Human progress, including through governments and their policies, is possible, but failure and regression are also ever-present possibilities. One must avoid a triumphalism that expects a great and perfect society will be created by our own efforts. (See Gen. 3:6, Rom. 3:23, and John 3:17).

4.   Government has been established by God to promote a just order in society that benefits the common good. Governmental authority and rulers are a part of God's benevolent provision intended for the good of all persons in a fallen world. Governments ought to seek to pursue justice for all, whether that involves punishing those who have violated the rights of others or promoting justice for those who have been denied opportunities to be what God wants them to be as his image bearers and for those whose enjoyment of the fruits of their labors are threatened. Public policies ought not to be evaluated by how they affect one personally or certain segments of society, but by how they affect the common good. (See Rom. 13:4 and Deut. 16:18–20).

5. The institutions of civil society are important. In between individual persons and governments are a host of civil society institutions and structures, including families, religious congregations, neighborhoods, voluntary associations, health-care and human service agencies, and many more. These civil society institutions and structures are a part of God's ordering of society; therefore, governments and their public policies ought to protect the appropriate freedoms of these institutions, avoid weakening and undercutting them, and work with and strengthen them as appropriate. (See Gen. 2:18–24, 1 Sam. 10:19, and Matt. 22:21.)

The six contributors were also presented with a set of "Guidelines for Respectful Conversation" (see the first section of Appendix A) and were encouraged to abide by these guidelines throughout this electronic conversation. The "Guidelines for Posting Comments" in Appendix A were also posted on my website as an indication of what criteria I would use to approve comments from APC readers on the submissions of the six contributors.

I believe we have accomplished our purpose of modeling respectful conversation to an admirable degree. During the nine-month duration of the APC project, the website had 23,388 page views and

7,774 unique visitors. The web activity has continued after the official end of the APC project with 30,181 page views and 10,223 unique visitors as of March 1, 2013.

More importantly, if you read through the postings of our six contributors on each of the twelve important public policy issues and through the comments posted by interested readers, two qualitative conclusions clearly emerge.

First, the conversations were indeed respectful. Contributors engaged in some strong disagreements about controversial issues yet demonstrated a deep level of respect for those with whom they disagreed. Contrary political opinions were expressed with deep conviction but without calling into question the integrity or motives of those with different views.

Second, we demonstrated that when people who situate themselves at various points on the political spectrum respectfully share their positions on difficult public policy issues, it is possible to identify some common ground in the midst of their differences and to illuminate their differences in a way that opens the door to the possibility of continuing the conversation.

Although I have quoted only a few of the comments from my APC readers in this book, a careful online examination of readers' comments about the contributor postings reveals that they added important perspectives to our conversations. Of the 162 comments submitted by APC readers, I rejected only one submission and that because it was submitted anonymously.

I believe that anyone who reads the full electronic transcript of postings by the contributors and the posted comments from readers will conclude that this electronic conversation effectively modeled respectful conversation between evangelical Christians who disagree about important public policy issues.

The Next Stage: An Overview of This Book

To place the diverse views of the six contributors on twelve hotly debated public policy issues on the table (or more accurately, into cyberspace) was a formidable task, made possible only because of their hard work and faithfulness, for which I am most thankful.

But getting the contributors' diverse views into cyberspace is only the prolegomena to another formidable task: sorting through these points of view on each public policy issue to identify either common ground or "majority opinion" (where not all contributors agreed), to illuminate remaining disagreements, and to identify further questions that need to be addressed in the quest for uncovering even more common ground. I must turn to this second demanding task if I wish to exemplify the type of political discourse I believe politicians should practice if there is to be any hope for them to govern well. This book is devoted to that task.

In brief, the bulk of this book is devoted to my presentation of a synthesis essay for each of our public policy issues, in which I identify what I have uncovered as common ground (or majority opinion) among my contributors and pose questions for further conversation. The questions emerged either because of disagreements among the contributors or because they did not reflect on certain aspects of the issue being considered.

Believing that everything I read is seen through the lens of my interpretive framework, I understand the same will be true for you. Thus, I am open to the possibility that if you worked your way laboriously through each posting and comment on my APC eCircle, you might come up with a different set of synthesis essays. I certainly invite those who are not faint of heart to do so. But, for now anyway, you will be exposed to my attempts at synthesis. I can tell you that I have tried to minimize any distortions that could reflect my particular interpretive lenses by sharing first drafts of all of my synthesis essays with all my contributors, inviting their reflections on where I may have not done justice to their views and their readings of the views of their colleagues. I refined these first drafts accordingly.

Although I played a rather low-key role as moderator of the APC eCircle (submitting only a few of my own comments along the way), I have at times inserted a few of my own reflections in these synthesis essays; I believe that has been done in such a way that readers should be able to discern when I am sharing my own beliefs rather than reporting the reflections of the contributors. I saved some of my overarching beliefs about the various issues until the last chapter, which discusses the role of government.

It is important to emphasize that what you are about to read does not speak on behalf of all evangelical Christians. Rather, it reflects the views of seven evangelical Christians. If another group of evangelical Christians had undertaken this conversation project, the views expressed could have been significantly different. And, of course, there is no telling what the results may have been if this series of conversations had been carried out by a group representing a wide diversity of world views—religious or secular.

It is not the purpose of this book to promote the views expressed herein. Rather, the purpose is to *model* how engaging in respectful conversation about important public policy issues with people you disagree with can lead to uncovering common ground and sufficiently illuminate differences to allow ongoing conversation toward the goal of uncovering further common ground. The particular results of any such conversation can only emerge as we talk with those with whom we may disagree (since you cannot predict beforehand the results of a respectful conversation).

It will soon become apparent to readers of this volume that the issues we discuss are quite complex. Those looking for responses to complex issues that can fit into sixty-second sound bites or onto bumper stickers will be sorely disappointed. In fact, now might be a good time to stop reading. Of course, one of the primary purposes of this volume is to reject the simplistic sound bite/bumper sticker mentality that is so prevalent in the media, in the public pronouncements of our politicians, and among citizens. So I encourage you to read on.

I give the last words in this book to the contributors, without whom none of this would have happened. Each graciously agreed to write a closing reflection. My assignment to each contributor was rather open-ended: "Write a postscript that includes the following three elements":

- Your views on the current state of evangelical public policy discourse: What are its current strengths and weaknesses and how can it be improved?
- Your suggestion(s) as to possible viable strategies for evangelicals, and others, to motivate elected political representatives to engage in the type of respectful conversation that we modeled in our APC project.
- Whatever "final word" you would like to share as a result of your involvement in this project.

There are indeed many pearls of wisdom in their closing reflections.

Where Do We Go from Here?

Allow me to close this introductory chapter with my own reflections on where we can go from here. My vision for the future of political discourse is informed by the following "ideal" sequence for political deliberation and legislation.

- Politicians and citizens who situate themselves at all points along the political spectrum have equal opportunity to express their views on all public policy issues.
- When these various views have been expressed relative to each issue, further conversation uncovers common ground and illuminates differences and unanswered questions that call for further conversation.
- A subsequent round of conversation about remaining differences and unanswered questions uncovers further common ground while further illuminating remaining differences.
- This pattern of ongoing conversations is repeated until enough common ground is uncovered by citizens to enable them to present persuasive arguments to their political representatives, and enough common ground is uncovered by politicians to enable them to take appropriate legislative action

This ideal will surely be viewed as wishful thinking in our current political climate. But the electronic APC reported on above and the content of this book demonstrate that the first two steps can be accomplished by some concerned citizens who profess commitment to an evangelical expression of the Christian faith.

Therefore, my first hope for the future is that a significant number of evangelical Christians will embark on the third step noted above, using the synthesis essays in this book as a starting point for continuing the conversation.

Venues for this continuing conversation can include appropriate academic courses at Christian colleges and educational offerings at Christian churches. Allow me to offer one suggestion as to who should be included in such continuing conversations. The regular contributors to the electronic conversations examined in this volume are all political scientists, as we were focusing on the public policy aspects of the issues we discussed. However, as a reading of this volume will reveal, rich contributions were made by readers who are "working in the trenches" relative to the topics under discussion (e.g., in the chapter on education, note the contributions of those readers who are working in K–12 education). In that light, future conversations will be enriched if they include practitioners in the fields under discussion, as well as academics from other disciplines, because many of the key topics are interdisciplinary in nature.

Even more fanciful is my hope that many other U. S. citizens, whatever their world-view commitments (religious or secular), will become aware of this "better way" for political discourse that is being modeled by a significant group of evangelical Christians, and that will be sufficient to inspire them to embark on similar conversations in their respective spheres of influence. And my biggest dream is that this alternative political discourse will become so pervasive, like the proverbial snowball rolling down a hill, that our political representatives will come to see this alternative way of doing politics is the only way to get beyond the current partisan political gridlock and onto the only viable path toward governing.

I want all of my readers to understand why I am so deeply committed to the project of facilitating respectful conversations between persons who disagree with one another about important issues. My most foundational belief about what it means to be a Christian is to aspire to be a follower of Jesus, who summarized the essence of what such following means in his two great "love commandments": "you shall love the Lord your God with all your heart, and with all your soul, and with all your mind, and with all your strength . . . [and] you shall love your neighbor as yourself" (Mark 12: 30–31). I believe that a deep expression of my aspiration to love another person is to give that person a welcoming space to disagree with me on important issues and to then engage that person in respectful conversation about our disagreements, thereby opening up the potential for us to learn from one another. And I believe that my opening up such a hospitable space for others is also a deep expression of what it means for me to love God.

PUBLIC POLICY
ISSUES

The Federal Budget Deficit

Common Ground

The Status Quo on Expenditures and Revenues Is Unsustainable

In the words of Stephen Monsma, "If the present mix of revenue policies and spending patterns continues, federal budget deficits will continue to increase and the national debt will continue to balloon, leading in the future to a major fiscal crisis."

Amy Black concurs, saying that "deficits of more than a trillion dollars a year, our rapidly escalating national debt, and the exponential growth of entitlement spending create a fiscally unsustainable future."

As will soon be seen, agreement that we have a problem will not lead to unanimity as to the specifics of the best solution.

Everything Has to Be on the Negotiating Table

These words from Amy Black are accompanied by her proposal explaining what needs to be on the table for conversation: "Can we adequately reduce the current federal budget deficit by only enacting cuts in federal expenditures? No. Can we do it solely by enacting tax reform? No. The only way to address our current budget deficit problem is to rein in spending, revisit the tax code with the under-standing we likely need to increase some taxes, end many tax breaks and fundamentally reform existing entitlement programs."

Eric Teetsel agrees: "Resolving the deficit crisis will mean address-ing the agricultural subsidies, federal pay, defense spending, and more."

However, agreeing with this need for a "balanced" approach still leaves room for disagreement over the best "order" for addressing these various aspects of our deficit problem (more about that later).

Current Entitlement Programs Cannot Be Sustained

Although there is significant disagreement among the contributors about how to address the current imbalance between tax revenues and many federal expenditures, there appears to be agreement that the current Social Security, Medicare, and Medicaid programs cannot be sustained; major overhauls must be legislated. Eric Teetsel brings home the need for overhaul most powerfully when he notes the change in demographics from 1950 to 2000 that has led to "a 17-year increase in non-working years of retirees." The question remains as to which overhauls should be made.

Concern for the Poor Is Not Limited to Those on One Side of the Political Aisle

Debates about the federal budget deficit invariably include consid-eration of the responsibility that the federal government should or should not have in assisting the poor (an issue that will be dealt with in detail in a later chapter on poverty in the United States). But it is important to note that in this present conversation, all the contrib-utors, wherever their location on the political spectrum, agreed that Christians are called to address the needs of the poor. My own view is that it is a false stereotype to think that all those on one side of the political aisle are committed to addressing the needs of the poor while all those on the other side are only committed to increasing the wealth of the richest among us (although that can be true about certain elements of both parties).

However, agreement about the ultimate goal of assisting those who are living in poverty is a far cry from agreeing about the best means for reaching that goal. In oversimplified terms, those on one side of the aisle lean toward viewing the free market as the best means for addressing the needs of the poor, while those on the other side of the aisle tend to believe that significant governmental programs are needed for those who do not fare well in a free-market economy. These contrasting tendencies will come to the forefront below.

Questions for Further Conversation

Unanswered questions abound, reflecting either disagreements among the contributors or aspects of the federal budget deficit problem that were not addressed in our Alternative Political Conversation.

Which Strategy Should Be Pursued First, Cutting Expenditures or Increasing Revenues?

Two of the contributors argue that priority must be given to cutting expenditures. David Gushee asserts that "The American people must in principle first cut spending, then raise taxes, then hold both steady," he says, by "learning to pay on time and in full for the services we wish to purchase from our government." While granting that steps must be taken to cut expenditures and increase revenues, Eric Teetsel asserts that "the most critical issue is entitlement spending."

My own view is that cutting expenditures and increasing revenues must be addressed at the same time, for two reasons. First, all budgeting, from the home to Washington, DC, involves choosing priorities, on both the income and expenditures side, and such choices reflect value judgments that are interrelated.

Furthermore, given that the nature of politics is for those on both sides of the aisle to advocate strongly for their particular priorities, it is even more naïve than I tend to be to think that when those who focus on cutting expenditures are satisfied, they will then cooperate in seeking legislation that will increase revenues, or vice versa.

What Is the Best Way to Increase Revenues?

An issue over which Republicans and Democrats have significant disagreement is whether tax rates need to be increased in order to increase revenues. As Stephen Monsma notes, one way of increasing revenues is to modify the existing tax code by "removing many of the current tax deductions, exemptions and write-offs now found in an overly complex tax code." This strategy for raising more revenues could conceivably be done without raising tax rates (although Democrats argue that such changes in the current tax code will not bring in sufficient revenue to cover needed governmental expenditures and that tax rates on the wealthy will also need to be increased).

In response to Democrats' ideas to raise taxes on the wealthy, Republicans argue that such taxes will penalize job creators, thus causing an adverse effect on the economy. Besides, they argue, the best way to increase revenue is to expand the economy rather than to raise taxes.

In his response to Nathan Berkeley, one of our APC readers, Stephen Monsma suggests there is a prior question: "Are current federal tax rates so high . . . that they stifle (or would stifle) economic growth, or are they low enough that raising them would yield additional revenue without stifling economic growth?" Monsma believes "taxes can be raised—or, more accurately, go back to an earlier level [prior to the Bush tax cuts]" because "historically the economy has grown and prospered when tax rates were higher than they are now." Monsma cites the 1980s (during the latter Reagan years), and the 1990s, during the Clinton years, as examples. Because this is a historical claim, further conversation needs to cite empirical evidence.

What Should Be Done about Military Spending?

Two of the contributors explicitly call for a reevaluation of military spending. David Gushee questions whether we want to continue to spend 20 percent of the federal budget "to continue to buy the largest and most expensive military in the world." Lisa Sharon Harper supports "the present administration's moves to make the military more efficient, nimble, and cost effective." More conversation is needed, especially in light of our consideration of later topics related to foreign policy.

How Should Entitlement Programs Be Overhauled?

Despite agreement that current entitlement programs cannot be sustained, the contributors arrive at no consensus as to how best to overhaul these programs. Various proposals are on the table. David Gushee suggests the need for means-testing for benefits. Stephen Monsma suggests that "changes in social security could include making some of the payments means tested for future retirees."

Given the changes in demographics of senior citizens, Eric Teetsel suggests that "Americans can—and should be expected to—work longer," adding that "means testing is an additional potentially beneficial reform." Similarly, Amy Black suggests that "we have to confront the changing demographics of our aging populations and longer life spans by gradually increasing the age of eligibility for Social Security and Medicare."

The contributors offer various proposals for cutting the spiraling costs of Medicare and Medicaid. As a precursor to some proposals that will emerge in a later chapter on health care, Stephen Monsma suggests that we need to "move away from the strict fee-for service system and towards various forms of managed care systems," noting the Cleveland Clinic and Mayo Clinic, where doctors are on salary and not paid according to services they provide or the number of tests that are ordered, as "examples of the possibility to control health care costs without reducing the quality of care."

Eric Teetsel notes that "a significant portion of Medicare spending occurs during the last year of life." Discussion of the implications of that fact will no doubt be lively.

How Can the Social Safety Net be Made More Efficient?

Lisa Sharon Harper suggests that "while it is true that America has a social safety net, it is weaker than it was just forty years ago," and says those who embrace "family values" need to avoid nullifying programs "that protect at-risk American families from slipping into poverty." However, David Gushee suggests that "we must review our spending on the 14% of the budget that provides a safety net for the poor, with the bias toward finding more efficient ways to meet the same needs."

Wayne Sweitzer, one of our APC readers, asserts that there is "a moral (and spiritual) obligation on those who are rich to help those who are poor," but also believes that "the federal government is the least qualified organization . . . to define, mandate, and enforce such obligation." This issue of who is best able to help the poor will be raised again when we get to the topics of poverty in the country and the role of government.

What Is the Meaning of "Justice," and How Is that Meaning Related to Addressing the Problem of the Federal Budget Deficit?

The question regarding the meaning of "justice" comes up in a number of our conversations, concluding with reflections in our last conversation on the role of government.

For now, Paul Brink suggests the possibility that "justice requires that all members of society have the ability to participate in our common life," adding that if his assertion is the case, then "the cost of efforts to reduce the deficit may not be borne by the most vulnerable members of society." This view of justice seems to inform Amy Black's assertion that "in the interest of justice, we must maintain a progressive tax system that asks those who benefit the most to contribute the most." David Gushee tempers Amy's assertion somewhat by proposing that "taxes should be progressive but not confiscatory and cannot be loaded onto the backs of any one portion of the population."

In Paul Brink's response to APC reader Lindsey Arnold, he points to at least one of his reasons for believing that justice requires all members of society to have the ability to participate in our common life: "the meaning of justice . . . is more than simply procedural—that is concerned with more than maintaining fair 'rules of the game.' Rather, justice is also restorative—it seeks to restore what is broken, working to always regain the righteousness that originally characterized God's good creation." Hence, Brink adds that "a properly designed social welfare system should have as its purpose not simply the bare sustenance of those who are poor—that is to provide resources to keep people alive, clothed and housed. Rather justice demands we do those things so that people can be restored to community, that they can be enabled to contribute to our common life."

How Can We Navigate the Tension between Economic Stewardship and Justice?

Expounding upon his view that justice "requires that all members of our society have the ability to participate in our common life," Paul Brink points to the tension between that "moral claim" and the moral claim that we exercise "economic stewardship," which entails not living beyond our economic means.

David Gushee suggests that economic stewardship requires that we "pay on time and in full for services." Further discussion will be needed as to how to navigate this tension.

Is "Shared Sacrifice" Called For? Is It Politically Feasible?

For politicians to propose that citizens may have to sacrifice to contribute to the well-being of others is like stepping on a third rail. So, Amy Black is swimming upstream when she suggests that "sound fiscal policy needs to start with the principles of wise stewardship and shared sacrifice," adding that "government programs and services benefit us all, and we all have an interest in maintaining a stable and well functioning system." But, "given current budget realities, we will all need to make sacrifices to ensure future stability."

It is my view that all who aspire to be followers of Jesus should be prepared to make appropriate sacrifices—although much conversation will be needed about the nature of such sacrifices. But I like to think that the idea of making certain sacrifices to promote the common good will resonate with many persons of goodwill, whatever their world view, despite the hesitancy of their political representatives to ever hint at that possibility.

Immigration

Common Ground

The Current System of Immigration Laws Is Broken

Although the contributors situate themselves all across the political spectrum, it appears there is consensus that the current system of immigration law is broken and needs some type of repair. As Amy Black says: "Even in this highly-charged political climate, there is widespread agreement that the current immigration system desperately needs repair."

The contributors also share commitment to the overarching principles that can inform attempts to fix the system, which are presented below.

The God-Given Dignity of Every Human Being Must Be Respected

This agreement is not surprising since, before this conversation started, all the contributors agreed on a set of "Basic Christian Principles for Politics and Public Policy." One of the shared beliefs in that set of principles is that "All human beings are created by God and in his image." Paul Brink asserts that "justice may not mean treating everyone alike, but it will require the recognition that all persons have dignity," and reminds us that "this dignity comes not from the possession of a passport."

The Rule of Law Must Be Respected

None of the contributors evidence disregard for the rule of law. They agree that it is appropriate to "punish" those who have broken the law, including those immigrants who have entered our country illegally. Of course, the nature of the "most appropriate punishment" is much debated (more about that later). But Stephen Monsma reminds us that "Undocumented immigrants are not the only ones breaking the law." Employers who knowingly hire undocumented workers have also broken the law and should be held accountable.

The Stranger and Alien Must Be Welcomed

As pointed out by both Stephen Monsma and David Gushee, this principle is clearly articulated in both Testaments of the Bible, from the call in Leviticus 19:33–34 for the people of Israel to "love the alien living with you . . . as yourself" to the words of Jesus in Matthew 10:40: "Anyone who welcomes you welcomes me, and anyone who welcomes me welcomes the one who sent me."

Paul Brink views the call to welcome the stranger and alien as a special case of a "justice mandate" to "take special steps to protect the most vulnerable." While all the contributors embrace this call to welcome the stranger and alien, there appears to be some disagreement as to the most appropriate nature and possible limits to that welcome.

Churches Should Demonstrate Love to Their Immigrant Neighbors

As Amy Black puts it: "Our churches need to be out front sharing God's love with our immigrant neighbors," being "centers for compassion-based ministries such as English language classes, tutoring programs, evangelism and outreach, counseling, food pantries, and health and dental clinics," and even making provision for legal services. Although not all of the contributors expressed that belief, it would be surprising if any of them would disagree. But the question as to whether such ministries are sufficient is still open to debate.

It is one thing to agree on overarching principles. However, as we will see, that agreement on principles doesn't guarantee finding common ground regarding the specific implications of these principles. But the postings of the six contributors reveal that some common ground also emerged in drawing out implications of these principles, as seen in the material that follows.

The Unity of the Family Must Be Protected and Fostered

A strong concern expressed by most of the contributors was the devastating effect that current immigration law has on the stability and unity of families of immigrants. As Stephen Monsma notes: "Our current immigration laws are rife with injustices, often separating husband from wife and or children from parents." Paul Brink suggests that because of their vulnerability, "children of illegal immigrants require special protection," and "something like the DREAM act is likely to be an important step in that regard."

In a follow-up conversation, Lisa Sharon Harper noted the devastating "breaking up of families" that the mass deportation of undocumented immigrants would bring about, "separating mothers and fathers from their U.S. citizen children."

I can testify that in a series of meetings on immigration issues I led in my home church in northwest Iowa in the fall of 2011, when we Anglos listened to the painful stories told by some of our immigrant neighbors and talked with our neighbors (not at or about them), the most prevalent theme in these stories was the devastating effect that current immigration laws were having on the stability and unity of their families. This should cause politicians on both sides of the aisle who talk a great deal about "family values" to sit up and take notice.

A Strong Guest Worker Program Must Be Established

The contributors appear to agree that a strong guest worker program that provides at least "temporary" work for immigrants is necessary. Eric Teetsel suggests that "low-skilled immigrants . . . contribute to the American economy in an important way," adding that a guest worker program would "meet the demand for low-skill immigrant labor" and even proposing that consideration be given to "a 21st century version of the Bracero guest worker program". The context of Teetsel's proposal is his observation that "comprehensive immigration reform has proven to be a political minefield," but he believes "there are some smaller fixes that can be done in the meantime."

Similarly, Stephen Monsma observes that "most immigrants fill low-wage and low skill jobs that employers otherwise have a hard time filling." He adds that "there are many American employers who need low-wage workers with the strong work ethic that many . . . [immigrants] have."

Amy Black suggests that "current immigration policy offers few, if any options for poor laborers to enter the United States legally to meet labor needs essential for economic growth."

In a follow-up conversation, Lisa Sharon Harper takes one step further the argument that immigrant labor contributes to economic growth, citing the projection of "experts" that "expanding Temporary Worker programs would . . . add 792 billion to the GDP over 10 years." But if the country really wants to focus on economic growth, she notes that these same "experts" say if "the U.S. could enact comprehensive reform with an earned path to full legal status, . . . 1.5 trillion dollars would be added to the U. S. GDP over the next ten years." Lisa is clearly calling for comprehensive reform now, not temporary fixes with the hope that comprehensive reform will happen some day.

National Borders Must Be Secured

Not all of the contributors address this issue. But it appears that none would disagree with the need to secure national borders. Paul Brink presents the positive case most strongly when he asserts that "[nation] states have the authority—and indeed the responsibility—to police their borders," adding that "[nation] states need to be concerned about cross-border criminal activity, including human trafficking."

However, from the overall content of this conversation, it is obvious that none of the contributors would support a one-dimensional approach to immigration reform that focuses exclusively on the need for border security. Rather, they view taking more appropriate steps to strengthen the security of our borders as one component of a multifaceted approach to reforming immigration law.

Majority Opinion

A Path to Legalization Must Be Created for Undocumented Immigrants

None of the contributors agree with the "loud voices" that "brashly call for just shipping all the illegal immigrants [approximately 11 million] 'back where they came from.'" Solely on practical grounds, before more important moral considerations, this is "inconceivable and impossible," according to David Gushee.

Eric Teetsel does not address the issue of a possible path to legalization for undocumented immigrants, possibly because he questions the political feasibility of large-scale immigration reform. However, the other contributors call for creating a path to "legalization" (albeit not necessarily "citizenship"). Paul Brink suggests that such a path to legalization (and he adds "citizenship") should focus on those "who have long been here, working and contributing to society."

This is not to suggest an "easy path." In a follow-up conversation, Lisa Sharon Harper calls for an "earned path," and the result should be "emergency temporary legal status," with the undocumented immigrant obtaining such temporary status then getting "at the back of the line (behind documented workers already seeking citizenship) to enter the process of obtaining full legal status."

In addition to noting the obvious requirement to pay back taxes, Stephen Monsma suggests that "criminal background checks" are needed to "weed out those whose behavior demonstrates that they should not stay here" (by virtue of having committed crimes or by demonstrating "unsocial behavior"). He further suggests that "legalization could include some kind of requirement not just of paying taxes going forward, but also a requirement to pay extra taxes for a period of time to help communicate the gravity of having broken immigration law in the first place."

Paul Brink suggests that this path to legalization should be open to those illegal immigrants who have "been here a long time" and who are "working and contributing to society."

As the above proposals reveal, advocating for a path to legalization for illegal immigration is not necessarily arguing for amnesty, as is often suggested by those who oppose creating such a path. Strictly speaking "amnesty" means "no punishment." The contributors are proposing that some form of punishment—short of deportation—is appropriate. The obvious unanswered question is: What form of punishment is most appropriate? The contributors have not found common ground in response to that question.

Questions for Further Conversation

Are Church "Caring Ministries" for Immigrants Sufficient?

It is fair to say that the contributors believe that church caring ministries for immigrants are necessary. But none of them argue that such
compassionate services to our immigrant neighbors are sufficient.
They would argue that—in addition to, not in place of—such church
ministries, Christians should be addressing what they perceive to
be systemic evils, such as a broken system of immigration laws. But,
whereas the contributors appear to hold this view, many Christians
do not, so further conversation will be helpful.

Should Immigration Reform Be Piecemeal or Comprehensive?

Whereas the majority of the contributors believe comprehensive
immigration reform would be ideal, it seems they hold out little hope
that such proposals will gain any traction in our current political
climate. But all the contributors agree that even piecemeal reform
is desirable, and even possible. But it is legitimate to ask whether
the time and energy spent seeking piecemeal reform could be better
spent mobilizing Christians to advocate for the ideal now, not later.

*Are There Limits to the "Welcome" that Christians Should Extend to
Immigrants?*

On the surface, the call to Christians to welcome immigrants seems
unconditional. David Gushee states this most boldly: "Our Christian
identity should yearn for a world in which everyone (at least, everyone
who poses no threat to anyone else) is welcomed anywhere they want
or need to go." But Paul Brink seems to qualify this claim with his
assertion that "[nation] states need to make decisions concerning the
number of immigrants they can accept." What are the implications of
this apparent disagreement for those churches that wish to provide

sanctuary to immigrants who enter the United States illegally? This leads to a related question.

What Is Legal?

Amy Black asks: "Is it legal to serve and help immigrants, regardless of their legal status?" She even suggests that "because of ambiguous statutory language, the legality of providing transportation can be a gray area." To complicate matters further, a related issue (not raised by the contributors) is whether Christians have an obligation to obey existing laws that they believe to be unjust. When, if ever, is "civil disobedience" called for?

What Is Fair to Taxpayers?

Based on a call for Christians to treat all people justly, Amy Black notes that "while millions of undocumented workers pay significant taxes," according to a recent Congressional Budget Office report, "these tax revenues do not fully offset the total cost of government services undocumented workers and their families receive." What is our reaction to her suggestion that "Federal law should redistribute revenues in ways that help states bear this financial burden?"

If a Path to Legalization Is Provided for Undocumented Immigrants, What Is an Appropriate Punishment for Their Having Broken the Law by Entering the United States Illegally?

As already noted, whereas most of the contributors believe that some form of punishment is appropriate, they are far from agreeing what that form of punishment should be. None of them argue for deportation of all undocumented immigrants. What, then, is an appropriate middle ground between deportation and no punishment?

Should English Language Proficiency be Required for Obtaining Legal Status or Citizenship?

David Gushee proposes that "it is reasonable for . . . legislation [toward some kind of comprehensive immigration reform] to impose an English language proficiency requirement to anyone seeking to become an American citizen." He further suggests that "churches should offer . . . resources for free English language instruction."

In a follow-up conversation, Lisa Sharon Harper suggests that a "path to EARNED legal status or citizenship" should include a "requirement to learn English." The other contributors do not address this issue. Should a distinction be made between language requirements for legalization and language requirements for citizenship?

I personally question the need for this language requirement based on my boyhood experience, as my mother, an immigrant from Norway, was a "good citizen" but would have had trouble passing an English proficiency examination. Possibly a "pass" should be given to those who nurture their children to be good citizens.

Are U.S. Trade and Domestic Policies Contributing to our Problem with Undocumented Immigration?

This question is all-too-seldom asked. Lisa Sharon Harper suggests that "America's highly subsidized corn put corn farmers in Mexico out of business," since "they couldn't compete with America's artificially low prices," thereby contributing to the desire of many Mexicans to move north to subsist. She concludes that "our government is a large part of the reason why Mexico's economy has tanked over the past 30 years." For Christians concerned about addressing systemic evil, this raises some important questions for further conversation.

How Do You Keep Employers from Illegally Hiring Undocumented Workers?
Stephen Monsma suggests that "with a wink and a nod," some employers "hire undocumented workers, while knowing many must indeed be undocumented." The "word on the street" in northwest Iowa suggests that Monsma is correct. There is no easy foolproof solution to this problem. The present E-Verify program for confirming the legal status of job applicants is riddled with problems, such as outdated databases, and often defeated because of the ease of obtaining forged documentation. Monsma suggests that "all immigrants, whether permanent residents or temporary guest workers, should be issued a tamper-proof identity card, and severe penalties should be established for employers who hire workers who do not have such cards." Monsma adds that the cards "could be made tamper-proof by way of modern technology such as embedded microchips." Much further conversation is needed.

Religious Freedom

Common Ground

Separation of Church and State Does Not Exclude Religion from Public Discourse

As articulated by Stephen Monsma, the phrase "separation of church and state" refers to "church" and "state" as "two formal organizations or institutions" that should indeed be "separate," "with the state not attempting to take on the duties of an organized church and the organized church not attempting to act like the state."

But Monsma also asserts that such legitimate separation at the organizational level does not exclude religion from public discourse because "all of us . . . whether deeply religious or more secularly minded—are shaped in our thinking and policy positions by our beliefs, backgrounds and life experiences."

In my own words, the inevitability that our world-view beliefs, whether religious or secular, inform our public policy positions calls for an "even playing field" where citizens and politicians alike should have the freedom to explain how their world-view beliefs inform their positions without imposing their world-view beliefs on others.

It can be argued that this view of the "separation of church and state" accords with a proper understanding of the First Amendment stipulation that "Congress shall make no law respecting an establishment of religion, or prohibiting the free exercise thereof." Echoing Stephen Monsma, Lisa Sharon Harper notes that this First Amendment clause "stands in favor of the non-establishment of a single religion over all, yet does not seek to form a secular state through the exclusion of religion altogether from public discourse," thereby protecting the rights of a plurality of religions. Eric Teetsel adds that "the relevant principle inherent in the Constitution is that vibrant and active religious communities are good for society."

Religion Is Not Private

None of the contributors embraces a narrow view of the meaning of religion that limits religious expression to what takes place in a home or a meeting of a religious congregation. As noted by one of our readers, Nathan Berkeley, such a truncated ("enlightenment") view of religion "reduces it to something less than a comprehensive way of life that should be operative for its adherents in all spheres of life and should take many institutional forms." In responding to Berkeley's posting, Amy Black notes that a proper view of religion "includes beliefs, identity and practice."

It is my view that President Obama's administration was assuming an inadequate, overly narrow view of religion as limited to the private sphere when it made its decision requiring birth control coverage to be provided in health insurance plans for employees. The administration exempted churches from the Department of Health & Human Services (HHS) mandate but did not provide exemptions for faith-based organizations such as hospitals, schools, and social service agencies, even though many such entities view their provision of services as deep expressions of their religious commitments (more about that later).

There Are Limits to Religious Freedom

None of the contributors assert that freedom of religious expression is without limits. But no consensus emerged as to the nature of the boundaries, which leads us to the first of some thorny unanswered questions.

Questions for Further Conversation

What Are Appropriate Limits to Religious Freedom?

Amy Black's view on the limits to religious freedom is indicated by her support of "the legal test created in *Sherbert v Verner* ("since abandoned") that "laws that interfere with religious practices are only allowed if (1) the state can show it has a 'compelling interest' for creating the law (the highest standard of scrutiny to justify the need for a law), and (2) that state cannot achieve its goal any other way without hindering religious observance." Of course, both components of this test involve judgment calls that will elicit disagreement.

Stephen Monsma suggests that it may sometimes be appropriate for the government to issue broad "mandates" that inadvertently limit the religious freedom of certain individuals or groups, noting the examples of a military draft, the refusal of unemployment benefits to someone who refuses to take a job that involves working on the Sabbath, and the levy of heavy fines against a faith-based organization that does not accede to the aforementioned Obama administration mandate to include birth-control coverage in health insurance plans for its employees.

Monsma notes that simply doing away with mandates in these three cases hypothetically could "have negative consequences for the common good"—"a nation's military may not have the military personnel it needs to protect its people, unemployed workers may destroy the unemployment insurance program by turning down offered jobs, and abortion rates, women's health, and dysfunctional families may increase if birth control is less readily available." Stephen Monsma argues that conflicts between public policies the government has concluded are necessary and the religious freedom of persons and organizations have usually been—and should be—resolved by creating exemptions for those whose religious beliefs clash with the public policies.

Whatever test is used, David Gushee proposes that "the burden of proof is a very high one, and it rests entirely with the state, to demonstrate why this or that exceptional case requires the overriding of religious liberty." But, once again, much conversation will be needed since well-intentioned persons may disagree over the terms of the test. Needless to say, such conversation must take place on a case-by-case basis. I will illustrate this by noting the positions the contributors have taken relative to the HHS mandate concerning contraception services.

Is the HHS Mandate Relative to Contraception Services a Violation of Religious Freedom?

A majority of the contributors judge that the HHS mandate that faith-based organizations include birth control coverage in health insurance plans for their employees is a violation of religious liberty.

Eric Teetsel asserts that this HHS mandate is "clearly out of bounds."

Amy Black asserts that the HHS mandate is "an unacceptable violation of religious liberty," adding that "at a minimum, the Department of Health and Human Services should offer religious organizations an exemption from directly or indirectly paying for services or medications that violate their religious beliefs and doctrine."

Stephen Monsma seems to be arguing for an "exemption" when he expresses his "hope that we as a nation will follow our historic precedents that have created religious exemptions for persons and organizations in religious traditions that have long-standing, thought-out, faith-based objections to legally imposed mandates."

David Gushee does not take a position on this issue, other than proposing that the state has a "high burden of proof."

On the other hand, Lisa Sharon Harper embraces the amended version of the HHS mandate, asserting that "by requiring insurance agencies to pay for [contraception] service directly, and not the institutions themselves, the administration preserved religious liberty and the disestablishment of religion." However, reader Nathan Berkeley calls into question this amended version when he suggests that "insurance companies mandated to cover contraceptives at no cost to their customers will inevitably pass some or all of those contraceptive costs onto the employers."

Nathan Berkeley also questions the HHS mandate based on his belief that "access to free contraceptives does not impact women's health in such a way as to justify violating religious freedom." Of course, there are many women and men who would argue that access to free contraceptives does impact women's health to such a significant extent that no exemptions should be granted to the HHS mandate on religious freedom grounds.

These differing views regarding the HHS mandate clearly point to the need for ongoing conversation. But Paul Brink raises the ante by proposing an oft-neglected question relative to the nature of religious freedom, which will be explored next.

What Kind of Freedom Should Be Granted to Religious Organizations?

Brink calls into question the "narrowly individualist view of religious freedom" that is characteristic of the "liberal version of constitutional democracy." Not only does this "individualist" focus lead to the narrow view of "religion as private" (which all our contributors reject, as noted above), but is also fails to acknowledge the "rights" (even "religious rights") of "institutions" and the responsibility of the state to protect such institutional rights.

In that light, Paul Brink finds the "the language of 'exemption' . . . troubling because it suggests that those who understand faith in a non-liberal way are merely to be tolerated by the rest of us." He concludes that "genuine respect for pluralism demands that liberalism, Catholicism, nationalism, secularism all be denied pride of place, and that our polity be understood to embrace *all* who reside in a territory, regardless of race, religion, gender and all the other distinctions that divide" (since "pluralism is here to stay").

Amy Black implicitly shares Paul Brink's view that organizations, not just individuals, have "rights" when she indicates that she "strongly supports the right of faith-based organizations to consider religious beliefs and religiously-based behavior when hiring employees who are essential to key religious activities and for communicating the faith."[1]

The issue that Paul Brink raises relative to the "rights of organizations" leads to another unanswered question.

---

[1] In the 2012 Hosanna–Tabor Evangelical Lutheran Church and School v. Equal Employment Opportunity Commission case before the Supreme Court, lawyers from the Obama administration sought to deny church-run schools a longstanding exemption from anti-discrimination laws meant to safeguard religious schools' freedom to hire and fire employees according to their own faith-based criteria. The Court reaffirmed the exemption.

Should Tax Dollars Go to Faith-Based Organizations that Provide Social Services?

Not all of our contributors address this thorny question. But enough is said to inform further conversation. Amy Black advocates "permitting government policies that might result in aid to organizations (religious or secular), as long as the policies neither favor nor promote religion."

In contrast, David Gushee indicates that whereas he "once supported this funding stream [of tax dollars to faith-based organizations providing social services] because of its benefits for the common good," he is "now wondering whether it was ever a good idea." Pointing to the "vexing legal difficulties, such as the hiring policies of religious organizations whose hands touch tax dollars," he observes that "in retrospect, those religious institutions that have avoided contact with federal money look exceptionally wise." More conversation is obviously needed.

Syria and Iran

It was difficult to identify significant common ground among the six contributors as to the foreign policy stance that the United States should take relative to the situations in Syria and Iraq. Although the reasons for that difficulty are not directly addressed by most of our contributors, I resonate with Amy Black's suggestion that as we seek to formulate a "Christian response," we "can start by admitting that we can't fully understand the depth and complexity of these issues nor can we easily predict outcomes of the array of possible responses governments may pursue."

John Hubers, a reader who served for many years as a missionary in Bahrain, applauds Amy's recognition of "complexity, suggesting that one element of this complexity is that any discussion of Iran's nuclear weapon build-up "cannot remove Israel from the equation."

However, despite this complexity, some common ground, as well as one area of majority opinion, did emerge.

Common Ground

Human Beings Are Fallen, and We Live in a Broken World

The statement of "basic Christian principles for politics and public policy" that all six contributors agreed to before beginning the APC conversations included the assertion that "human beings are both fallen and capable of redemption." The postings of the contributors on the Syria and Iran situations suggest that U.S. foreign policy should be informed by their shared belief that all human beings are fallen. But, even though the contributors believe no one lies beyond what God is capable of redeeming, including the former Iranian President Mahmoud Ahmadinejad, none of their position papers suggest U.S. foreign policy should be directly informed by that redemptive possibility.

Rather, I believe it is fair to say that all of our contributors would agree with Stephen Monsma's assertion that we live in "a sinful and broken world" where "there are always going to be dangers, threats, and injustices," and this undeniable brokenness places limits on the steps that can be taken through public policy to ameliorate such dangers, threats, and injustices.

From this bit of "Christian realism," Monsma concludes that "our goal as a nation ought not to be to create a utopian world where evil regimes no longer exist and international threats are a thing of the past," adding that such a misplaced goal "would lead to a never ending stream of wars and bombing campaigns as we seek to right wrongs around the world." This assertion will eventually lead us to a few thorny questions.

The Options for U.S. Involvement in Syria and Iran Are Agreed Upon

The collective postings of our contributors identify the following options for U.S. involvement in Syria and Iran, ranging from "soft power" to "hard power" options, although as the Majority Opinion section below will reveal, there is no unanimity as to which of these options should be exercised. The options include:

- Humanitarian assistance
- Cultural and economic ties
- Exemplifying freedom and democratic ideals
- Diplomatic negotiations
- International isolation
- Economic sanctions and pressures
- Military force.

Majority Opinion

Military Involvement in Syria or Iran Is Unwise

Although there is no unanimity among the contributors as to which of the above options ought to be exercised, a majority argued for some sort of "soft power."

Paul Brink favors sanctions in the case of Iran. The military option in Iran may meet the "just cause" criterion in "just war" theory, Brink asserts, because of the "nuclear danger, but also because of Iran's demonstrated support for international terrorist organizations." However, he says it fails the three just war tests of "proportionality of ends" (the good achieved by the use of force must be greater than the harm done), "reasonable hope of success," and "last resort." Brink also judges that "military intervention in Syria would be unwise" because of concern about the "prospects for success" and lack of clarity as to "whether the good of the end is proportional to the harm that will result."

David Gushee asserts that we should not intervene militarily in Syria or Iran, but should rather "join with many nations in provid-ing humanitarian assistance" in the case of Syria and "international isolation" in the case of Iran.

Using just war criteria, Stephen Monsma judges that "it is dif-ficult to justify military action in the Syrian situation." Although he believes that "the situation in regard to Iran, when compared to Syria, poses greater dangers and the case for military intervention is greater," he also believes that "military action should not be taken," concluding that "United States' soft power may be more effective than the hard power of military action." He believes "economic sanctions are beginning to have an impact on Iran, and further sanctions . . . have the potential of having even a bigger impact." Monsma also proposes that "containment may be an appropriate strategy relative to Iran's development of nuclear weapons," which will be discussed in more detail below.

Eric Teetsel asserts that Mahmoud Ahmadinejad "is an evil man" and bemoans the "naiveté and . . . mistaken tendency of some Christians to avoid confrontation with evil." While noting with approval the "non-violent effort" of Martin Luther King to "get involved in the fight for racial justice in America" and recognizing that the movement "went far beyond mere dialogue," Teetsel says, "I don't know what the United States or our allies should do to confront Iran," and "I don't know the best way forward on Syria (or Pakistan, Russia, France or Canada for that matter)." But "hoping for the best is not a strategy. Blithely disregarding warning signs of evil and instability will only lead to suffering and death. The United States is a leader with unparalleled influence. Our burden is to stand for what is good and combat what is evil, one way or another."

Amy Black suggests that "the United States has few, if any, viable options for a unilateral response" to the Syrian situation, noting that "experts generally agree that the extensive complexity on the ground precludes most military options."[1] She concludes that "the United

---

[1] One of the "complexities on the ground," for the Syrian situation, as well as for the Israeli/Palestinian conflict addressed in the next conversation, is the difficulty in identifying exactly who the "players" are. In the case of Syria, which groups comprise the opposition to the al-Assad

States, the Arab League, the United Nations and others should continue seeking solutions and pursuing diplomacy, but we should not expect a quick and easy end to this crisis."

With respect to the nuclear threat posed by Iran, Black says, "we could engage in more direct diplomacy and hope that those efforts combined with increased sanctions result in Iran allowing inspectors into their sites." She guardedly allows for the possibility of the United States initiating "some sort of limited military action," noting that "successful [air] strikes could set a weapons program back two or three years." Finally, Black proposes that the United States needs "to assess if we can live with a nuclear Iran," suggesting that "some strategy for containment may be possible."

Lisa Sharon Harper does not directly address the Iran situation. But in the case of the Syrian conflict, and potential future conflicts in other nation-states, she presents a proposal that reflects painful lessons learned from Croatia and Iraq, saying "talk of military intervention . . . must come only after the following three conditions have been met":

- Any action the United States takes to intervene in conflicts within another nation-state's borders must be with the express consent of the U.N. Security Council.
- Any action the United States takes to intervene in conflict waged within another nation-state's borders must NOT be a unilateral action. The strengths of institutions such as NATO, the Arab League, and the U.N. Security Council must be utilized to make them full partners in a multilateral action.

---

regime, and who provides leadership for and "speaks for" the opposition? The answers to these questions appear to change over time.

- Military action is always a last resort. Every possible means of diplomatic action must be taken before the threat of war is uttered.

Questions for Further Conversation

Numerous thorny questions lie beneath the surface of the above narrative.

Is Containment a Viable Strategy Relative to Iran's Nuclear Program?

Amy Black suggests that "we need to assess if we can live with a nuclear Iran. Although this is not a preferred scenario, building a bomb does not automatically lead to using it. Some strategy for containment may be possible."

Similarly, Stephen Monsma says,

> if worse comes to worse and Iran does develop nuclear weapons, it is far from clear that containment and a nuclear standoff with Israel and the United States would not work. Such a standoff between the United States and the old Soviet Union for some 40 years did not lead to nuclear war. Such a standoff is far from ideal and must grieve any person committed to Christ's call to be peacemakers. But, in an imperfect, broken world prudence suggests it is a lesser evil than military action by the United States that would surely result in many human deaths and injuries.

Is containment a viable strategy, or are the differences between the leadership of the old Soviet Union and the leadership of Iran so great as to preclude such a strategy?

What Are Appropriate Criteria for "Just Humanitarian Action?"

A number of the contributors appeal to just war criteria in assessing whether military action is justified relative to Iran and Syria. But as

Paul Brink astutely points out, these criteria do not work well when trying to assess the justification, or not, of "armed humanitarian intervention into states." For example, relative to the just cause criterion in just war theory, Brink notes that "self-defense and collective security are the only just causes under international law."

In that light, Brink states that "my first impulse with regard to the Syrian case is to appeal for more good theoretical work to be done on the matter of *just humanitarian action*" (italics mine).What are appropriate criteria for justifying such military action on humanitarian grounds? Brink suggests that the just war criterion of "right authority" may "provide guidance," adding that "the United Nations role as the institution capable of determining violations of collective security (its 'chapter 7' powers) may provide grounds for asserting its place as the 'right authority' for justifying military intervention on humanitarian grounds." This suggestion leads us into what may be the most fundamental unanswered question.

What Are Appropriate Uses and Limits of U.S. Power?

David Gushee observes that "recent years have shown the limits of our power and the increasing costs of attempting to exercise it." This sober observation calls into question our tendency as Americans to want to "go it alone."

As the above narrative reveals, Paul Brink, David Gushee, Amy Black, and, especially, Lisa Sharon Harper explicitly point to the need for multilateral action, not unilateral action, relative to the situations in Syria and Iran. Of course, a common objection to multilateral strategies is that we could be thwarted by the intransigence of these "other players" and, besides, we know what is "good," which leads to two further thorny questions.

Are Multi-Lateral Conversations Called For, Including "Talking with our Enemies?"

David Gushee suggests that for both the Iranian and Syrian situations, "we should keep lines of communications open even with regime leaders whose behavior is odious—not because we like them or endorse them, but because that is the best way to advance our own interests and the interests of the citizens of those nations."

Eric Teetsel takes a polar opposite position, calling into question those Christians (especially pacifists) who "naively believe that men like Ahmadinejad can be reasoned with." Teetsel especially criticizes David Shenk, a Mennonite scholar, who apologized to the president of Iran "for President Bush's failure to engage him in dialogue."

I would go even one step further than David Gushee, by asserting that Christians should engage in respectful conversation with anyone who disagrees with them, not simply because of the good results that may emerge, although that would be welcomed. But this act is necessary because creating a welcoming space to express disagreements, even with a person considered to be an enemy, is a deep expression of what it means to love that person, which is what Jesus has called all those who claim to be his followers to do. And I dare to propose that engaging someone who disagrees with you in a respectful manner is an appropriate action for all human beings, whatever their world-view commitments, religious or secular, because of our common humanity.

There may indeed be some wisdom in the words attributed to Moshe Dayan: "If you want to make peace, you don't talk to your friends. You talk to your enemies."

This sounds terribly naïve when it comes to the Iranian and Syrian situations. But have we adequately tried orchestrating respectful conversations with the leaders in Iran and Syria? I read about a willingness to talk with the leaders of these regimes provided that certain preconditions are met. But to set preconditions for the "results" of a conversation is a charade since *you cannot predict beforehand the results of a respectful conversation* (which is the deepest conviction that informs all of my work these days). Despite my passion about this conviction, I could be wrong. So, further conversation is needed.

Who Is "Evil" and Who Is "Good?"

Eric Teetsel asserts that "Mahmoud Ahmadinejad is an evil man." Steve Monsma asserts that "both Syria and Iran are evil regimes." I believe that both of these judgments are correct. But the Christian principle that "all human beings are fallen" precludes the possibility of us judging that any one person or regime is "totally evil" or "totally good."

The clear biblical teaching is that every human being has the capacity for doing evil and doing good,[2] as does every regime. So, whereas, as noted by David Gushee, "we [Americans] have believed that we *are* good and *ought to pursue good* in the world," there is ample evidence, in our personal and national lives, that we are not always good.

The United States has a well-documented history of supporting regimes that wreaked havoc on its citizens. John Hubers, one of our readers, points to the fact that "in 1953 Iranians elected a president in a free and fair election. Our CIA then orchestrated a coup to replace that government with a despot whose CIA trained secret service had a well deserved reputation for being the most brutal in the region."

---

[2] This dual human capacity for good and evil was famously pointed to by Aleksandr Solzhenitsyn in *Gulag Archipelago*, "The line separating good and evil passed not through states, nor between classes, nor between political parties, but right through every human heart."

If one grants that all persons and regimes are capable of doing evil and doing good, that assumption will inform the substance of the possible multilateral conversations suggested above and would seem to suggest that all possible efforts at exerting soft power must be exhausted before even considering the possibility of military action. However, a segment of the Christian community would preclude ever taking military action, as the next question suggests.

What about the Pacifist Option?

Guided by just war theory, none of the contributors rules out the possibility of military action in Iran or Syria, albeit only as a very last resort after all attempts at "soft power" have been tried and failed. But there are Christian pacifists who would rule out military action at any time or under any circumstances. These Christians should also be provided a welcoming place at the table in all ensuing conversations about Iran and Syria.

I aspire to be a peacemaker, but I am not a pacifist in that, influenced by the example of Dietrich Bonhoeffer, I cannot rule out in the abstract the possible need for resorting to military action in unusual cases of "tragic moral choice." In such cases, all the available options are destructive of kingdom-of-God values, and one must choose the "lesser of evils." For interested readers, I elaborate on that position in my book *Learning to Listen, Ready to Talk: A Pilgrimage Toward Peacemaking.*[3]

---

[3] Harold Heie, *Learning to Listen, Ready to Talk: A Pilgrimage Toward Peacemaking* (New York: iUniverse, 2007), 137–154.

Israel and Palestine

Amy Black asserts that "the Israeli-Palestinian conflict is a tragic example of the complexities of geopolitics," which echoes her opinion on the "complexity" of the Iran and Syria situation.

However, Stephen Monsma suggests that "most observers are convinced that the path to a peaceful resolution of this [Israeli-Palestinian] conflict is not shrouded in mystery." He adds that "although the specifics would need to be worked out through a long and difficult process of negotiation, the general outlines of the only peace agreement that seems workable are clear." Monsma then proposes four main components of such a peace agreement. Similarly, Paul Brink and Amy Black suggest some necessary elements of a peace agreement.[1]

Although there is some overlap between the proposals offered by Monsma, Brink, and Black, I cannot point to one proposal that reflects common ground. Therefore, I will create a composite proposal that draws from the three but is not identical to any one, and present it merely as a hypothesis that will require further conversation.

---

[1] Eric Teetsel did not post on this topic.

Hypothesis for Discussion

A peace agreement between Israel and Palestine will need to include:

- Establishment of a viable and sustainable sovereign Palestinian state in the West Bank and Gaza to exist alongside the state of Israel.
- Either removal of all Israeli settlements from the West Bank or a "land swap" (i.e., some adjustment in the pre-1967 borders so that some Israeli West Bank settlements would become part of Israel and the Palestinian state would receive some Israeli land in exchange).
- Recognition by the international community and Israel's neighbors of the legitimacy of a secure Israeli state.
- Allowing a limited number of Palestinians (or their descendants) who were displaced either when the state of Israel was created or due to the 1967 Six-Day War to return to their original land and giving financial compensation to other Palestinian refugees either from Israel or an international fund created for this purpose.
- Dividing Jerusalem between the Israelis and Palestinians such that neither party will have sovereignty.

It is conceivable that this composite hypothesis will not be embraced by Stephen Monsma, Paul Brink, or Amy Black, not to mention other readers of this book. So, much further conversation will be needed.

Questions for Further Conversation

Even if Israelis and Palestinians could agree to the broad terms of a peace agreement like that proposed above, to imagine that this agreement regarding basic contours could be followed by agreements spelling out specific details and modes of implementation appears to be a flight of fancy. Why is that? Some of the unanswered questions below will try to get to the bottom of that overarching question.

Can Conflicting Claims to "Divine Establishment" Be Reconciled?

Paul Brink cogently points out why the Israeli-Palestinian conflict seems to be intractable: "If there is any area of the world where history matters, it is Israel-Palestine. In a region where ties to the land are frequently *divinely established,* it can be hard to establish the conditions for compromise" (italics mine).

It is virtually impossible to see things from the perspective of the other side when you are convinced that God is on your side. The only way I can see to get beyond that impasse is if both Israelis and Palestinians are able to appeal to teachings in their respective traditions that counter any claim that God is exclusively on their side. Seeking to uncover teachings about "justice" in these two great traditions may be a place to start.

What Does Justice Require?

Stephen Monsma asserts that "justice [is] essential to peace," adding that "the problem is not that no one knows the way forward [to a peace agreement]. The problem, rather, is finding among the leaders and populace of both sides the will, the courage, and the commitment to a balanced justice essential to peace." According to Monsma, this means "justice for both the Israelis and the Palestinians."

As in the conversation on the federal budget deficit, the challenge is to arrive at agreement of the meaning of "justice for both sides." I personally embrace an adaptation of the definition that Paul Brink proposed in that earlier conversation: "justice requires that all members of society have the ability to participate in our common life." I believe this adapted definition is appropriate for the Israeli-Palestinian conflict: *justice for both the Israelis and Palestinians requires that both groups be enabled to live safe and secure lives in which each group will have the opportunity to flourish.*

My proposal for what would be a just resolution of the Israeli-Palestinian comports with my evangelical Christian faith commitment. But a way forward in the present conflict will be found only if Israelis and Palestinians can uncover teachings in their respective traditions that embrace some version of this concept of justice that is compelling enough to counter any claim that God is on their side exclusively.

Surely there are injustices perpetuated on both sides in this conflict. My own indirect exposure to one such injustice came when I received a phone call one early morning in the mid-1990s from the director of the Christian Peacemaker Teams informing me that my son Jeff (who was serving with the CPT in Hebron) had been detained by the Israeli Defense Force for the "crime" of accompanying a water truck to the residence of a Palestinian family.

In light of my son's experience, I resonate with the following call from Lisa Sharon Harper for "empathy" from the Israeli populace: "It is time for the state of Israel to look into the faces of every Palestinian and see itself. There was a time when Israel was a people without a land. There was a time when the Hebrew people had their property confiscated and their families separated. There was a time when they were disowned by the world."

Of course, practicing empathy is a two-way street. For any hope for peace to materialize, Palestinians also have to make every effort to "put themselves in the shoes" of the Israelis in a manner sufficient to understand their experiences of injustice.

Can the United States Be a "Neutral" Facilitator toward a Peace Agreement?
Paul Brink answers with a resounding "no." In his own words,

> When parties to a negotiation are unequally matched, a
> hands-off policy permits the stronger party to dominate the
> other. And let us be clear: the parties in the Israel-Palestine
> conflict are unequally matched. Palestine consistently enters
> into negotiations with a dramatically weaker power position.
> This has any number of consequences, but chief among them
> is that the United States cannot act as a "neutral facilitator"
> and hope that the negotiation process will be seen as legiti-
> mate by the Palestinian side.

Based on his experiences living in the Middle East for many years, one
of our readers, John Hubers, concurs with Paul Brink's response. He
asserts that "the Palestinians have come to recognize that America
cannot be an honest broker in this conflict."

In a response to Hubers, Stephen Monsma points out that the
United States has helped to broker peace in the Middle East, citing
the roles of President Carter in the 1978 Camp David Accord, and
President Clinton in the 2000 Camp David Peace Summit. But he
acknowledges that there is a "pro-Israel bias in American Policy over
the years." Monsma elaborates by asserting that "currently, American
efforts seem to be guided more by calculations of American self-interest, pressures from the American Israeli lobby, and other domestic
political calculations." To Monsma's description, I would add "pressures from the Christian Zionist lobby," a topic that will be discussed
more later.

If one grants that there has been a pro-Israel bias in U.S. policy
regarding the Israel-Palestine conflict, what steps can be taken to
rectify that bias? Amy Black asserts that "although I believe that

our commitment to Israel is well warranted, I don't think it should be unquestioned." Black calls for "more meaningful dialogue about what our role should be in the region," adding that "American diplomats and political leaders need the political space to weigh various options." I personally embrace Black's call for a "space for conversation," but with the proviso that all the relevant voices be invited to the table, which raises an important question as to the nature of a potential evangelical Christian voice.

What Can the Voices of U.S. Christians Contribute to a National Conversation on the Israel-Palestine Conflict?

It is my view that our national conversation about U.S. foreign policy relative to the Israeli-Palestinian conflict has received an unbalanced contribution from Christians in the United States. The "end-times dispensationalism," which is one way of interpreting biblical prophecies, pointed to by David Gushee teaches that the return of Jesus Christ at the end of times is contingent on the Jewish nation returning to their promised land. This has led to unwavering, unquestioned support for the state of Israel, come what may, on the part of some Christian Zionists.

But there are alternative Christian voices, including those of a number of the contributors to this book, that have not been adequately heard. For example, Stephen Monsma asserts that "American evangelicals err when they read biblical prophecies in a way that leads them to put unwavering support for Israel ahead of justice for Israelis and Palestinians alike." Reader John Hubers, puts it even more bluntly, bemoaning "Americans supporting injustice in the name of Christ."

I think it is tragic that many Christians choose to ignore the clear biblical teaching that those who claim to be followers of Jesus should seek justice for all peoples. American evangelicals who share this conviction need to gain a greater voice in the national conversation regarding U.S. foreign policy with respect to the Israeli-Palestinian conflict.

Lisa Sharon Harper expresses a strong alternative voice when she dares to question the prevailing "war paradigm" where "there are only friends and enemies; those who are like the self and those who are threats to the self." As Harper points out, "the war paradigm is not the paradigm of Jesus' Sermon on the Mount. It is not the paradigm of the Cross. And it is not the paradigm of *Shalom.*"

In stark contrast to the war paradigm, the concept of *shalom*, which Harper describes as a "Hebrew concept grounded in the book of Genesis and woven throughout every book of the bible from Genesis to Revelation," embraces the possibility of harmonious and peaceable relationships between all peoples.

To those who find such lofty aspirations for shalom to be laughable in our broken world, I point to one long-standing initiative that has taken some first steps toward fostering it between Israelis and Palestinians. The Seeds of Peace Camp in Maine brings together Israeli and Palestinian teenagers to talk to each other about the nature of the conflict and explore possible ways to get beyond the current intractable impasse.

I had the privilege to visit the Seeds of Peace Camp one summer in the late 1990s, when my son Jeff and his wife, Tammy Krause, were serving as counselors. The conversations were intense, but a small ray of hope emerged when the teenagers from these two warring traditions actually got to know and befriend one another as fellow human beings. The hope was that some "seeds of shalom" had been sown that could one day bear fruit on a large scale across their traditions. This leads me to a final question that some would be consider to be outrageous.

Can Seeds for Peace Be Sown on the Ground instead of in the Halls of Power?
David Gushee makes an important distinction between "absolutists" and "pragmatists," noting that there are absolutists in both the
Israeli and Palestinian populations, those who "yearn for total occu-
pation of every square inch of the land between the Jordan and the
Mediterranean." He adds his dual perceptions that Israel's "population appears to be slowly swelling with absolutists, many imported
from the United States," and that "Israel today has the misfortune
of being led by a governing coalition that contains a too sizable rep-
resentation of the absolutists."

But the ray of hope that Gushee points to is that one can also find
pragmatists on both sides, those who "have come to terms with the
need to share the land between the two populations." How can the
number and influence of these pragmatists be increased?

I believe more pragmatists will emerge on both sides if more
concrete steps like the Seeds of Peace venture are taken to enable
both populations to get to know one another better, to befriend
one another. Those ventures can thereby open up the possibility, as
suggested by Lisa Sharon Harper, of the emergence of a sufficient
degree of "mutual empathy" to set in motion initiatives that exemplify
shalom. Is it possible that a significant increase in grass-roots move-
ments could mobilize many Israelis and Palestinians to work together
for shalom and that such compelling examples would motivate the
political leaders on both sides to work toward terms of agreement
for a lasting peace?

Poverty in the United States

The fact that the level of poverty in the United States is increasing cannot be denied. As noted by Stephen Monsma, in the fall of 2011, "the Census Bureau reported that the number of our fellow Americans living in poverty had increased for the fourth consecutive year. It found that 15 percent, or 46 million persons, are living in poverty, up some two and a half million persons in one year."

Lisa Sharon Harper notes the disparity in poverty rates between whites and blacks: "According to the 2010 census, 25.4 percent of blacks and 11.1 percent of whites are living below poverty."

Stephen Monsma also provides data to support the fact that "poverty rates and a stable, healthy economy are closely related," noting the four years of increasing poverty mentioned above "coincides with the fallout from the 2008 financial crisis and the resulting recession. During the years of a relatively strong economy from 1993 to 2006 the poverty rate fell from 30 percent to 21 percent." However, Monsma adds, "even with a strong economy . . . many are still left stuck in poverty."

Do these statistics move us? Paul Brink asserts that "the fact that poverty continues to be found within America is an offence against the gospel." Lisa Sharon Harper "wants to know when American politicians of this age will weep over poverty in America."

Common Ground

There Are Multiple Causes of Poverty

The contributors recognize the complexity of the problem of poverty is due in part to its multiple causes, including the exploitation of the poor by the wealthy, the existence of systemic and institutional problems, and in some cases, laziness.

A number of the contributors point to structural changes in the American family as a significant cause for the increase in the level of poverty. Steve Monsma asserts that much of the persistent poverty can be traced to "the breakdown of the family," citing the "telling statistic" that "in 2010, of families composed of a married couple only 6 percent were poor; of families headed by a single woman 32 percent were poor." David Gushee concurs, adding that the "dramatic rise in the numbers of children being raised by single parents, especially single mothers, has led to documented disadvantages for those children."

The quality, or not, of the upbringing of a child also has a profound effect on the future security, financial and otherwise, of the child. Eric Teetsel brings this point home powerfully when he contrasts his own experience of the "support of loved ones" that eventually contributed to his financial stability with the story of a child whose parents were addicted to methamphetamine: "when social workers finally rescued the girl, she was eating the raw meat of a deer carcass left on the dining room table."

Christians Are Called to Alleviate Poverty

There is no doubt among the contributors that Christians have a responsibility to help alleviate poverty. For example, Stephen Monsma says, "The Bible contains thousands of references to the poor and our responsibility not to ignore them, but to offer them our help. In Matthew 25 Christ teaches that we will be judged by our response to those who are naked, hungry and sick. An active concern for the poor is not optional for the Christian."

Paul Brink argues that the involvement of Christians, and others, in alleviating poverty is a matter of doing justice: "those who are not poor have a duty not only to care for those who are poor, but also to speak for their cause, to advocate for change wherever they have influence, and in other ways to advocate—and vote—for economic justice for all."

Multiple "Actors" Must Work to Alleviate Poverty

David Gushee suggests that "every sector of society has a responsibility to address both long-term structural poverty as well as the more short-term spreading of that poverty upwards to the middle class," citing possible roles for "churches . . . businesses . . . and legislators."

While recognizing some role for government, Eric Teetsel suggests that government cannot replace the role of "parents, grandparents, siblings and cousins," further noting "the necessity of intact families, churches and other social organizations to positively influence the lives of the poor."

There Is a Role for Government in Alleviating Poverty

Although Eric Teetsel warns that Christians should not "subcontract our charitable witness to the government," all the contributors recognize that government should be one of the "actors" in the quest to alleviate poverty, although there is no common ground as to what its role should be. Several reasons are given for such government involvement.

Amy Black points to the sheer magnitude of the problem of poverty. She asserts that while "charitable work is essential . . . it is rarely enough to deal with the underlying problems of poverty," adding that "meeting immediate needs is necessary, but it will never be sufficient to combat the structural and institutional problems that contribute to domestic poverty."

Similarly, Paul Brink asserts that "some of the causes of poverty are structural, and often it will take government action to deal with structural injustice."

Stephen Monsma rejects the "either/or" options that the major political parties often present, with some Republicans asserting private actions and the work of civil society institutions such as churches and other community-based programs are all that is needed, while some Democrats say government-initiated and government-run programs would be sufficient. In sharp contrast, Monsma says it must be both: "both government actions and actions arising from individuals and civil society institutions are needed."

One of our readers, Nathan Berkeley, called into question Steve Monsma's "both/and" proposal based on the principle of "subsidiarity" that is prominent in Catholic social teachings, which implies that "provision for the poor should be handled by the social institution that is smallest and closest to the poor that is capable of handling it." Monsma responds that, while such efforts are important (the second pole of his both/and proposal), they are "often inadequate," adding that "poverty is a complex, multi-faceted problem with multiple causes. To deal with root causes and not merely symptoms, often longer-term more persistent efforts and greater financial resources are needed than a family, church, neighborhood, or locality is likely to possess."

Both Stephen Monsma and Paul Brink suggest a subdivision of responsibilities between government and private/community actors that reflects their respective strengths and weaknesses. In Brink's words," "Government programs are blunt instruments, and evidence suggests that other actors in civil society can be much more effective at providing material and non-material assistance to those in need." Monsma suggests that "churches and faith-based and other community-based organizations have advantages the government does not have" when it comes to providing the "training in basic life skills and changes in attitudes and behaviors" that are needed to alleviate persistent poverty.

Our Efforts to Alleviate Poverty Should Foster Growth toward Self-Sustenance rather than Dependency

Eric Teetsel points us to a very important distinction between the "short-term" poverty of "someone whose temporary life circumstances have resulted in insufficiently adequate income to meet basic needs" and the "long-term" poverty of "someone whose inability to provide for themselves is, essentially, permanently fixed." Based on this distinction, he asserts that government services should focus on helping poor individuals to move from "positions of temporary poverty to self-sustenance."

Similarly, Amy Black asserts that the goal of "public assistance programs" should be to help the poorest Americans "without creating a culture of dependence." In that light, Black proposes that government assistance programs should "encourage work and pathways to permanent and stable employment" through job-training programs and should "provide incentives helpful to the working poor," such as the earned income tax credit, transportation assistance, and subsidized childcare.

Questions for Further Conversation

What Is the Proper Balance between Private/Community Actions and Governmental Programs for Alleviating Poverty?

Considering the problem of poverty highlights the importance of the distinction in the political realm between forging agreement as to desired "ends" and then reaching agreement as to the best "means" to accomplish those ends. Many politicians and citizens of good will, be they religious or secular, agree on the desirability of minimizing poverty in the United States. But they debate fiercely over identifying and employing the best means to accomplish that worthy end.

The APC contributors favor the both/and approach that utilizes some combination of the efforts of institutions of civil society (e.g., families, churches, community organizations) and governmental involvement. However, they disagree on the best balance between these two approaches, and ongoing conversation needs to address this question of balance.

When seeking this optimum balance, effectiveness should be taken into account. In his response to reader Nathan Berkeley, Stephen Monsma bemoans "too many Republicans simply wanting to cut programs for the poor, whether they are working or not, and Democrats wanting to increase spending on programs for the poor, whether they are working or not." More empirical study must be given to the effectiveness, or not, of both private and governmental programs.

My belief about an appropriate balance of responsibilities echoes Stephen Monsma's view that assistance programs that focus on the "human touch and transformative values of churches and other local organizations" are the most effective means for alleviating immediate poverty, but that significant governmental intervention is needed at the same time to address the systemic problems that lead to chronic poverty.

What Steps Can Be Taken to Alleviate the Poverty Caused by Structural Changes in the American Family?

Given the undeniable statistic that poverty is much more likely to occur in families headed by single parents, especially single mothers, steps must be taken to meet the considerable challenges faced by such parents. Such steps can include subsidized childcare and assistance in transportation to work sites that Amy Black has proposed. More far-reaching initiatives can include efforts such as counseling programs for families in distress to support the flourishing of families in the country. Should we reconsider the no-fault divorce laws that most states have passed? Are there steps government can take to strengthen the family? More conversation is obviously needed.

Should Tax Dollars Go to Faith-Based Organizations that Work to Alleviate Poverty?

Amy Black suggests that government should "encourage the participation of religious and community groups that serve the poor." But what forms should that encouragement take? Should it include financial assistance?

In elaborating on his both/and position that the task of alleviating poverty should involve both governmental involvement and private/community efforts, Stephen Monsma envisions a synergy that can "pair the financial resources of government (on the local, state, and federal levels) with the human touch and transformative values of churches and other local organizations" and asserts that with it, "we would have a powerful means to reduce poverty."

But the question remains as to whether such governmental financing should go to the faith-based organizations working to alleviate poverty. As already noted in the conversation about religious freedom, the question of whether tax dollars should go to faith-based organizations that provide social services is hotly debated, and no consensus emerges among the contributors.

Marriage

Majority Opinion

Marriage Is a Union between a Man and a Woman, but Same-Sex Civil Unions Ought to Be Legalized

With one exception, the contributors who posted position papers on this topic[1] argued for limiting marriage to unions between males and females, with Amy Black presenting the reason that "traditional marriage is a universal social institution created by God for the good of all humanity."

The one exception is Lisa Sharon Harper. As she reports in this electronic conversation, she has always "whole heartedly supported civil unions," but has in the past been "hesitant to support same-sex marriage." However, the process of writing a chapter on Same-Sex Marriage in her book *Left, Right & Christ: Evangelical Faith in Politics* "has been a convicting experience."[2] As she makes clear in her book, she now favors public policy that allows the same rights and privileges of marriage to same-sex couples as to all other couples. To

---

[1] David Gushee did not post on this topic.

[2] Lisa Sharon Harper and D. C. Innes, *Left, Right & Christ: Evangelical Faith in Politics* (Boise, Idaho: Russell Media, 2011).

do otherwise, she says, is to set up a legally sanctioned, two-tiered system of citizenship.

An important qualification to the majority opinion that marriage should be limited to unions between male and female couples is Paul Brink's question as to who has the right to decide "what is or is not a 'marriage.'" He raises the issue as to whether it would be better "to reserve [that decision] to other spheres of society" (not the state). I will return to this issue shortly.

Stephen Monsma indicates his support for legalizing same-sex civil unions, pointing us to "the wisdom of civil union laws that allow same-sex couples to live together with certain rights and responsibilities clearly and legally established," in addition to laws that "encourage monogamous permanent relationships."

It appears that the majority of the contributors would agree with Monsma's call for legalizing same-sex unions, with the possible exception of Eric Teetsel, who is concerned that "civil unions are an incremental step towards watering down the institution of marriage."

Common Ground

If the State Is to Define the Meaning of Marriage, It Should Do So in a Way that Promotes "Public Justice"

Accepting for now the definition of justice previously proposed by Paul Brink that "justice requires that all members of society have the ability to participate in our common life," I believe it is fair to say that all the contributors would agree that governmental policies should "do justice" to all couples, heterosexual or homosexual. However, as will soon be seen, agreement at this general level will not lead to unanimity as to what justice requires.

Given that the role of the state is to provide justice for all of its citizens, Paul Brink asserts that "when Christians consider same sex marriage as a public policy issue" we should not "approach the subject as if we were the church." Therefore, Christians who believe that homosexual acts are sinful should not advocate for public policy legislation prohibiting such acts because of that belief (remembering that only two of the proscriptions in the Ten Commandments have been prohibited by U.S. law).

Whatever the Definition of Marriage, the Civil Rights of All Persons Must Be Protected

As Eric Teetsel asserts, "no serious marriage advocate wants to limit rights of gays." Stephen Monsma points us to a reason that Christians have for protecting the civil rights of gay people: we should "treat those with same-sex orientation with the respect they as God's image bearers deserve."

Both Teetsel and Monsma enumerate some of the civil rights they believe ought to be extended to same-sex couples: inheritance rights, hospital visitation rights, shared property rights, and the right to reciprocal medical decisions.

Questions for Further Conversation

What Is the Purpose of Marriage?

Sociologists who study marriage from a cross-cultural perspective point out there is no single definition of marriage that takes into account the diversity of the human experience. Some of them even point out the complexity of the definition and practice of marriage in the Bible. One possible way to sort through various definitions of marriage is to reflect on the "purpose" of marriage. Our contributors present a variety of views, albeit with some considerable overlap.

Eric Teetsel embraces a view proposed by Sherif Girgis, Robby George, and Ryan Anderson in an article, "What is Marriage" in the

Harvard Journal of Law & Public Policy, that starts with a distinction between "two competing views of marriage: conjugal and revision-ist."[3] The conjugal view is that "marriage is the union of one man and one woman who make a permanent and exclusive commitment to one another that is naturally fulfilled by bearing and rearing children together."[4] The revisionist view is that "marriage is the union of two people who are romantically inclined to one another and care for each other, sharing the burdens and benefits of domestic life."[5]

These authors contend that "the conjugal view is the only one to uphold three widely held principles for what makes a marriage:" *"comprehensive union"*[6] (the marital relationship is all-encompassing including, crucially, bodily union (sex)); *"special link to children"*[7] (marriage itself is oriented to and fulfilled by the bearing, rearing, and education of children); and *"marital norms"*[8] (norms of perma-nence, monogamy, and exclusivity which create conditions suitable for children).

Amy Black quotes with approval the position taken by the late theologian John Stott as to the "three central purposes of marriage as outlined in Genesis: (1) the procreation of children and providing for the nurture and well-being of families; (2) the provision of suitable helpers who supply support, healing, and encouragement so that each marriage partner can recognize his or her full created potential; and (3) a reciprocal commitment of self-giving love which finds its nat-ural expression in sexual unity or becoming 'one flesh'." Black adds

---

[3] Sherif Girgis, Robby George, and Ryan Anderson, "What Is Marriage," *Harvard Journal of Law and Public Policy,* 34, No. 1 (Winter 2010), 245-287.

[4] Girgis, "What Is Marriage?" 246.

[5] Ibid.

[6] Ibid., 253-255.

[7] Ibid., 255-259.

[8] Ibid., 259.

her own view that "marriage is not about personal fulfillment; it is fundamentally about self-sacrifice and seeking the good of others."

Trying to create coherence from these various views will be a challenge, and some thorny sub-issues will emerge. For example, a focus on "procreation of children" seems to call into question the marriage of infertile couples, which I find deeply problematic. Furthermore, to imply that one must choose between "personal fulfillment" and the "seeking the good of others" seems to me to be a false choice.

These views also seem to presuppose that the proper nurturing of children is limited to heterosexual parents. Amy Black asserts that "as an institution, marriage . . . presumes that committed permanent male-female relationships are the best way (albeit not the only way) to protect and care for children." Her qualification ("not the only way") allows for the possibility that both single parents and same-sex couples can adequately protect and care for children. It is my understanding that some empirical evidence shows there are same-sex couples who provide loving environments that foster the growth and well-being of their adopted children in an exemplary manner.

But is there empirical evidence to support the premise that "committed permanent male-female relationships are the *best way* . . . to protect and care for children?" (italics mine). Recent empirical studies reveal that sociologists disagree about this question.

I believe it is fair to say that the various views on the purposes of marriage noted above are intended to support the overarching view that marriage should be between a man and a woman. That may be the case if all three of Stott's "purposes" must be satisfied. But I am open to the possibility of a couple having a "good marriage" when less than all three of Stott's "purposes" are satisfied. Many readers may disagree.

The above narrative outlines the views of various evangelical Christians as to the purposes of marriage. Those committed to other faiths, religious or secular, may hold differing views. That raises the question as to how one "does justice" to these varying views.

What Does Justice Require?

Based on his view that "from a Christian perspective, politics is fundamentally concerned with public justice," Paul Brink concludes that "justice demands that states offer recognition to same sex relationships, for the same reason that it recognizes heterosexual relationships: because the state has an interest in supporting stable familial relationships, and to provide the parties with the legal care that justice demands."

Elaborating, in turn, on these two "interests of the state," Brink asserts that (1) "the state has an interest in the ordered, stable reproduction of society. So generally the state will seek to encourage . . . stable relationships, especially because the state is concerned that children be raised in these sorts of loving environments"; and (2) "the protection of people within marriages and families will also be a concern of the state."

Amy Black at first appears to be on the same page as Brink, when, in response to his posting, she takes his assertion that "the state has an interest in the ordered, stable reproduction of society" to imply that "the state has a strong interest in protecting the institution of marriage as a union between one woman and one man." But Brink's position seems to allow for same-sex couples also providing the kind of stable "loving environments" the state wishes to encourage. Further discussion is needed regarding this difference.

It is my view that in our pluralistic society, it is unjust for federal or state government to impose on its citizens one definition of marriage that leads to one set of public policies relative to the possibility of same-sex marriage. Steps are being taken to legislate public polices regarding same-sex marriage, which raises the issue of how to deal with those persons or institutions who disagree with such legislation.

Given our Pluralistic Society, What Steps, if Any, Should Be Taken to Protect the Freedom of Individuals or Organizations Who Disagree with Federal and State Laws Allowing Same-Sex Marriage?

This question returns us to the thorny issue of "religious freedom" that was addressed in a previous chapter, in which Stephen Monsma argued that under most situations when the government issues a mandate that conflicts with some groups' religious beliefs and practices, it should provide for an exemption for those groups.

Monsma's test for whether a mandate is justified is if lack of a mandate will have "negative consequences for the common good." He then argued that in cases where it is judged that a mandate is necessary for the common good, it is important that individuals or organizations that have religious objections to the mandate be granted "religious exemptions."

Consistent with his stance noted above, Stephen Monsma now argues that "when states legally establish same-sex marriage it is essential that they include in the authorization language strong religious exemption language." He then suggests that religious exemptions should enable "churches not having to rent their facilities for a same-sex wedding, a Christian or Orthodox Jewish adoption agency not having to place children with same-sex couples, a faith-based college not having to allow same-sex couples in their married student housing units, and a small photography studio not having to take pictures for a same-sex wedding ceremony." These proposed exemptions no doubt reflect Monsma's judgment that granting such exemptions will not have significant "negative consequences for the common good," a judgment that other citizens may not share.

Because of this ambiguity as to when an exemption to a governmental mandate is appropriate, there appears to be no unambiguous, one-size-fits-all response to the question of what steps should be taken to protect the freedom of individuals or organizations who disagree with federal and state laws allowing same-sex marriage. That question will have to be answered on a case-by-case basis, making use of the collective judgment of legislators (and possibly the judicial system) as to the extent, if any, to which granting a religious exemption will have "negative consequences for the common good."

Should the State Get Out of the Marriage Business?

Paul Brink introduces this provocative question when, based on his views about the "proper differentiation of society" (differentiating the proper rights and responsibilities of the different sectors of society, such as the state, families, businesses, schools and churches), he suggests the possible need to "reserve to other spheres of society [other than the State] the authority to decide for themselves what is and is not a 'marriage.'" Brink is more direct when he adds that he doesn't think the state should "apply the label of 'marriage'" to same-sex relationships because "we should avoid the implication that marriage is somehow a creation of the state."

In their responses to Brink's posting, two of our readers pick up on his suggestion, albeit in more colorful language. Ramsey Michaels says "get the State out of the marriage business." Richard Pierard says that "as a firm adherent of the separation of church and state, I am extremely bothered by a minister acting as an agent of the State to solemnize contractual actions that are legal and secular in nature along with those that are spiritual."

As has been suggested by Tony Campolo and others, one possible scenario that would "get the state out of the marriage business" would be for the state to grant civil unions to all couples, heterosexual and homosexual, with all the associated rights and responsibilities. A given couple can then decide about "marrying" or not. If a secular marriage is desired, such arrangements can be made (e.g., asking a justice of the peace to perform the ceremony). A couple wishing to be married in a church, synagogue, mosque, or other faith-based congregation can seek out a congregation that would be willing to perform a marriage ceremony in light of its particular beliefs about the appropriateness of conducting heterosexual or homosexual weddings. In a response to Paul Brink, Amy Black points out that, on pragmatic grounds, our public policy seems to be headed in the direction of this dual possibility of "two definitions of marriage, one recognized by the state for civil purposes, and the other left to religious institutions to bless and define as they choose."

I think this scenario is worthy of further consideration because it justly allows for the diversity of views about the meaning of marriage that exist in our pluralistic society at the same time that it protects the civil rights of all couples, heterosexual or homosexual, who wish to make a lifelong, monogamous commitment to one another.

Eric Teetsel seems to applaud the fact that churches that differ with him about the meaning of marriage have the freedom to practice their particular views about marriage. In his own words, "there are many churches in America that joyfully 'wed' homosexual couples in ceremonies symbolic of their commitments to one another. Though I disagree with the behavior, I am pleased to live in a country where we are free to do that sort of thing."

Health Care

Common Ground

A Way Must Be Found to Provide Basic Health Care for All U.S. Citizens

In the words of Amy Black, "access to basic medical care is a right, not a privilege." Therefore, "advanced industrial societies should provide a way to provide basic health care for all of their citizens."

Stephen Monsma adds that this first principle is "rooted in a biblical concept of justice and concern for the common good." Lisa Sharon Harper suggests that the United States needs to offer its citizens "the health care worthy of every human being made in the image of God."

As will soon be seen, agreement regarding this desirable "end" leaves much room for disagreement as to the optimum means for attaining that end.

Spiraling Health-Care Costs Are Unsustainable

Amy Black points out that "the United States spends more money on health care per capita than any other country, and the rates of spending are growing faster than anywhere else," noting that "in 2008, the U.S. spent $7,538 per person," with Norway second highest at \$5,003. In 2010, "total health care spending in the U.S. was an astounding \$2.6 trillion."

None of the contributors argue that these spiraling costs are sustainable.[1] But, once again, no consensus emerged as to how best to break out of this spiral.

Questions for Further Conversation

What Is the Verdict on Obamacare?

As Eric Teetsel notes, the Obama administration's intent for the Patient Protection & Affordable Care Act (Obamacare) was "to solve the problem of coverage for those without access to insurance through existing means." However, Amy Black asserts that she is "not particularly impressed" with much of what she sees in the act because "the plan appears overly complex and deeply tied to our current system which most observers agree is broken."

To add a voice to that of the contributors, Dr. Timothy Johnson, former medical editor for ABC News, shares Black's concern when he gives "mixed reviews" to the Affordable Care Act in his provocative book, *The Truth About Getting Sick in America: The Real Problems with Health Care and What We Can Do*: "The good news is that the newly passed health care bill should eventually provide some kind of health insurance . . . to more than 30 million Americans now uninsured. The bad news is that the bill does not provide any assured way of controlling costs and guaranteeing quality."[2]

If Dr. Johnson's assessment is correct, a critical immediate question for further discussion must deal with possible strategies for

---

[1] David Gushee did not post on this topic.

[2] Timothy Johnson, *The Truth About Getting Sick in America: The Real Problems with Health Care and What We Can Do* (New York: Hyperion, 2010), 71.

controlling spiraling health-care costs. The question as to how to "guarantee quality" must also eventually be addressed.

Another aspect of Obamacare that Johnson applauds is the "insurance exchange" component, because "insurance companies will be competing for your business," which conservatives will like, and the federal government will "play a strong role in order to guarantee that all insurance companies play by the same rules and standards," which liberals will like. He sees this as a sensible partnership between government and private industry that is the only way to "get costs and quality under control."[3]

Is a Market-Based Approach to Health Care Adequate?

Eric Teetsel notes, with apparent approval, that "Republicans favor a market-based approach [to health care] that offers more flexibility and options to consumers by allowing individuals to purchase insurance from any state, deregulating the industry, and incentivizing innovative insurance products like Health Savings Accounts."

Teetsel does acknowledge that "the health insurance market has characteristics that distinguish it from other insurance markets and make it quite complicated as a matter of public policy." And he presents five examples that "demonstrate the complexity of public health," including the fact that "health is deeply personal" ("it can affect our whole lives and is often a matter of life and death"), and "health care is expensive."

Three of the other contributors question a purely market-based approach to providing health care. Amy Black notes that market strategies may work well for "elastic goods," where "if a price goes up demand goes down because consumers will substitute something

---

[3] Ibid., 39.

else in its place." But she notes that "inelastic goods are not affected by price changes; consumers will pay whatever price because such goods and services are necessities and have no substitutes."

Black quotes, with apparent approval, her professor in her first economics class in college using "health care as an example of something with a near inelastic demand curve." Amy adds that "when choosing a physician,, surgeon or cost of treatment, most of us ask first about quality, and expected outcomes" and that "cost is low on the list (or not even considered) when someone's life hangs in the balance." Her statement is consistent with Eric Teetsel's observation that one of the complicating factors in the provision of health care is that "health is personal."

Paul Brink agrees with Black's characterization of the "inelastic demand curve" for health care, as does Stephen Monsma, who says, "when it comes to health care market forces do not work well due to inelastic demand." As an illustration, Monsma asks, "When facing open heart surgery who wants to shop around for the cheapest surgeon?"

One of our readers, John Hubers, notes that "America is unique in its belief that health care should be treated as a marketplace commodity rather than a matter of public concern," suggesting that the public concern should be about "doing justice." He notes that some of his "Christian friends from Scandinavia often ask "How can Christians [in America] support this injustice? Why aren't you outraged?"

How Can Spiraling Health Care Costs Be Controlled?

What drives the escalating costs of health care? Amy Black notes that "experts disagree on the exact reasons for the high costs," but adds that "some of the contributing factors include the high cost of medical technology and prescription drugs, the expense of administering such a complex public-private hybrid system, overtreatment, and the increase in chronic illnesses."

Black points us toward at least one strategy for reducing health-care costs when she proposes that we must "seek alternatives to our current fee-for-service system that encourages unnecessary procedures and over-testing," a principle with which Stephen Monsma heartily concurs.

In the book cited above, Timothy Johnson strongly supports this principle proposed by Black. In his own words, the health care system needs to get away from "an ultimately disastrous financial incentive," whereby "the more you do [as a doctor or hospital] the more you make."[4]

For example, Johnson believes "we must pay all our doctors by salary . . . and a key component of that salary should be outcomes [not the number of procedures and tests that are ordered]."[5] He observes that "some of our best health care facilities, such as the Mayo and Cleveland Clinics, pay their doctors by salary in order to free them up from making decisions based on how much money they could make."[6]

This is not to suggest that doctors should be underpaid. Amy Black proposes as a fundamental principle that "medical personnel are highly-trained professionals who deserve reasonable compensation." Of course, there is much room for disagreement as to what constitutes "reasonable compensation" for doctors.

Based on her experience working in the health-care industry, Lisa, one of our readers, notes a complicating factor (also hinted at by Eric Teetsel) when it comes to the perceived problem of doctors ordering too many tests: "Doctors don't just order tests and procedures to

---

[4] Ibid., 15.
[5] Ibid., 18.
[6] Ibid., 18-19.

make money. Often they order them to insure that they don't miss something and get sued for extreme amounts of money."

Johnson acknowledges this problem, saying that "the specter of being sued makes many doctors pursue defensive medicine, and these indirect costs . . . [lead to] unnecessary expenses because 'it's better to be safe than sorry'." He reports the astonishing statistic (presented in the June 28, 2010 issue of the *Archives on Internal Medicine*)[7] that "91 percent of American physicians practice defensive medicine by ordering tests that are not medically necessary."[8] He proposes that "the only sensible answer to this royal mess is some sort of no-fault system—where *all* victims of injury, whether actual malpractice or not, are compensated according to living costs and projected lifespan through an impartial process using unbiased experts."[9]

Closing this section on a sobering note, Dr. Johnson is not optimistic as to the larger-scale possibility of cost-cutting measures gaining much traction because "the political and economic pressures (for jobs and profits) from the medical-industrial complex will override truly significant cost control."[10]

Should Health-Care Policy and Practice Place More Emphasis on "Outcomes?"

Amy Black observes that although "the United States is the undisputed center of medical innovation that paves the way for new drugs and devices," it doesn't rank as high in "positive health outcomes." She cites data showing that "in 2006, for example, the U. S. ranked

---

[7] Tara F. Bishop, Alex D. Federman, Salomeh Keyhani, "Physicians Views on Defensive Medicine: A National Survey," *Archives on Internal Medicine* (now JAMA Internal Medicine), 120, No. 12 (June 28, 2010).

[8] Johnson, *Truth about Getting Sick*, 27.

[9] Ibid., 27.

[10] Iid., 71.

39th [among nations in the world] for infant mortality and 36th for overall life expectancy."

Even more startling, Timothy Johnson reports that "many health care experts estimate that about a *third* of what we spend on health care in this country is unnecessary,"[11] meaning that the money spent doesn't result in better outcomes such as life expectancy and survival rates.

What would health policy and practice look like if there were more focus on the quality of outcomes? Could such a focus contribute to controlling health-care costs?

What Is the Role of Preventative Medicine?

Although our contributors did not directly address this question, the old saw that "an ounce of prevention is worth a pound of cure" could contribute to the controlling of health-care costs. This suggests the need for more wellness initiatives that promote exercise and good dietary habits.

To be more radical, Eric Teetsel wonders about the "morality of requiring society to subsidize costs associated with poor choices." That issue calls for further discussion, especially in light of disagreements as to "what constitutes a poor choice" and who should have the authority (or audacity) to make such judgments.

What Kind of Future Is Envisioned for Health Care?

Amy Black expresses her "current view" that "we need to move toward some form of single-payer health care delivery system that provides basic medical services to all Americans." She defines a "single-payer"

---

[11] Ibid., 28-29.

system as one in which all health care is funded from a single insurance pool, run by the government.

Stephen Monsma responds to Black by saying that "at some point we may conclude that a single-payer system is needed, but . . . if we ever reach that conclusion we should do so gradually, incrementally, and based on our experience with more modest steps." Monsma's basis for proposing this incremental approach is that "given human frailty, our limited knowledge, and the ever-present danger of unintended consequences—not to mention human perversity—there is much to say for an incremental approach to policy making in very complex areas such as health care."

In response to Monsma's response, Black proposes that we at least "need to move away from our current system of employer sponsored health insurance."

Based on his pessimism, as noted above, about the possibility of significantly controlling the spiraling health-care costs due to the current political and economic climate, Timothy Johnson makes a dire "big prediction" that will surely raise some eyebrows: *No matter what legislation Congress develops this year [2010] or in the years to come, health care costs will continue to rise. Within five to ten years, health care costs will be so out of control that we—the public—will demand that the government bail us out. At that point, the easiest and quickest action will be to expand Medicare to cover everyone*[12] (a public option [single-payer system] will be the only insurance choice for everyone).

Speculation as to the future of health care in the United States would be incomplete if consideration were not given to a lone opinion expressed by Thomas Major, one of our readers. In his comment,

---

[12] Ibid., 60.

Thomas, a disabled veteran, tells of his painful experiences with people working in his doctor's offices who don't even know his name. This leads to his "outside of the box" suggestion:

> Set up doctor's offices that work "like the good old days." Eliminate the complicated forms and standardized procedures that are very expensive, and not understood by most patients, and have a destructive effect on the doctor/patient relationship. The old fashioned office will work smoothly, at a profit, and no one will need to wait three weeks to be seen for a sore throat that is happening today. We don't even need to set up a committee or wait for an act of Congress to try this.

Health-care professionals may be tempted to scoff at the perceived "impracticality" of such a nostalgic suggestion. But if we ignore the spirit of this painful voice, which calls for a restoration of the "human touch" to the practice of medicine, we do so at our peril.

K–12 Education

Common Ground

There Are Some Significant Problems with our Current K–12 Educational System

The contributors agree there are some major problems with the current K–12 educational system in the United States.[1]

This is not meant to be a generalization applying to all schools because some schools and their students are flourishing. But too many schools, particularly in some large inner cities, are deteriorating and failing to adequately educate their students. Furthermore, comparisons of educational achievement of K–12 students from other countries reveal U.S. students are falling behind many of those students.

Some of the Problems with K–12 Education Are the Result of Poverty and Will Not Be Quickly Solved

Amy Black tells the poignant story of Paul, one of her students when she volunteered as a teacher's aide in a suburban California public

---

[1] David Gushee and Lisa Sharon Harper did not post on this topic.

school. On a field trip to the Los Angeles Zoo, she discovered that his "entire meal for the day" was "6 or 7 saltine crackers." In her own words, "as I quietly shared my lunch with him, my heart broke." She adds that "Paul arrived at our school sleep-deprived and hungry. His parents never attended a teacher's conference. He was failing 2nd grade, and life was failing him."

Black notes that "Paul's story is repeated over and over again across our country, and it emblemizes the problems that are at the heart of the education crisis. It is difficult to teach a roomful of students in the best of circumstances; the obstacles can seem insurmountable when students suffer from malnutrition, abuse, poverty or neglect."

She concludes that "we cannot achieve true educational reform without also addressing poverty and its damaging effect on children," citing the fact that "longitudinal studies reveal a significant, and rapidly growing gap in achievement between wealthier and poorer students that has lasting and devastating effects."

However, Stephen Monsma points out, "we will be waiting a long time" if we must reduce poverty before we can "correct the deep problems with our educational system." Therefore, he thinks some short-term, practical steps must be taken immediately.

Adding More "After School Programs" Is a Good Place to Start

The contributors applaud the effectiveness of after-school programs. Amy Black views such programs as an "important way to improve children's lives," by offering participants "a safe haven, filling the afternoon hours with sports, tutoring, healthy snacks, and fellowship."

Eric Teetsel and Stephen Monsma concur, with Monsma adding that participants in these programs "can receive the encouragement and help with their studies they too often do not receive at home."

He also reports that "in a number of focus groups I have conducted with teenage participants in such programs, they have described them as serving as a second family, with values, motivations, and role models they have not received from their own families." Monsma also suggests that providing such after-school programs "is where churches and other faith based civil society organizations can provide a vital service. . . . Something we can do that is positive and proven in effectiveness."

Questions for Further Conversation

The problems facing K–12 education are complicated by the fact that all levels of government (local, state, and federal) are involved in some way.[2] While the provision of K–12 education is primarily a state responsibility, elements of jurisdiction are delegated to local communities, and certain federal programs are available, such as a national school lunch program, financial assistance to local educational agencies for educating children of low-income families (the Title 1 program that was the precursor to No Child Left Behind), a drug-education program, and a special-needs program.

Funding for K–12 education averages about $9,000 per student per year. On average, about 50 percent of that total comes from state taxes, 40 percent comes from local taxes (e.g., property taxes), and 10 percent comes from the federal government. The complications caused by the subdivision of responsibility between local, state, and federal governments will become apparent in some of the following questions.

---

[2] I wish to thank Ron Juffer, professor of education at Northwestern College in Iowa, for giving me a much-needed tutorial on the intricacies of K–12 education, especially regarding the respective responsibilities of local, state, and federal government.

What Is the Primary Role of Government Relative to K–12 Education?

Paul Brink asserts that "government's interest in education [whether it be local, state, or federal government] . . . is ensuring that all children receive an education of reasonably high quality, and reasonably close to the wishes of the families receiving the education," adding that "the government interest is to support communities educating their children and doing so equitably."

This view of the role of government leads Brink to propose that "educational resources should be allocated among communities roughly in proportion to the number of students they are educating." This envisioned role for government implies the need to "insure that families living in underprivileged neighborhoods can access the same quality education that families living elsewhere are able to enjoy."

Remembering Brink's definition of justice ("justice requires that all members of society have the ability to participate in our common life"), his view of the role of government, as summarized above, would be an instance of government treating all its citizens justly.

Amy Black's way of supporting such a role for government is to say that "education is an essential public good that should be a priority for all—young or old, parent or childless—[since] it helps everyone in society gain essential skills they need to survive and thrive." The key words here are "public good" (not a "private good"). Since quality education contributes to the common good by preparing students for responsible citizenship, it should be supported by all citizens (parent or childless), primarily through appropriate taxing powers of government. (This is my response to the parents who complain about paying taxes to support their local schools even if they have no children attending these schools).

The ideas that the primary role of government is to insure that all students receive a high-quality education that is "reasonably close to the wishes of the families receiving the education," and that such education, under whatever auspices, contributes to the "public good" by means of a well-educated citizenry, leads to a thorny follow-up question.

Is a School Voucher System Viable and Desirable for K–12 Education?

In most parts of the United States, the funds collected for K–12 education, whether from local, state, or federal sources, goes directly to public schools. Those parents wishing to send a child to a private school pay tuition and other expenses directly to that school, in addition to whatever taxes they pay to support their local public schools. Paul Brink judges this practice to be "unjust" because parents who choose to send their child to a private school are then "paying twice."

An alternative to this current practice is some sort of school voucher system, in which funding for a portion or all of the expenses for educating a child is not given directly to a school. Rather, a voucher to cover a portion or all of the expenses is given directly to the parents of that child, who then choose the school, public or private, they want to educate their child, and transfer the voucher to that school.

Of course, going to a voucher system raises the question of whether granting vouchers to parents who then choose to use them at private, faith-based schools is a violation of the First Amendment to the U.S. Constitution.

As Stephen Monsma reminds us, the Supreme Court has already ruled that "vouchers can be used at Christian and other faith-based schools without violating the Constitution," provided certain requirements are met, as is the case in existing pilot programs in Milwaukee, Cleveland, and Washington, DC.

The debate over the viability and desirability of a school voucher system for K–12 education is heated. On the pro side, Stephen

Monsma argues that a school voucher system that allows parents to choose the school to educate their child, rather than insisting that the child go to a local, dysfunctional, public school, will enable families living in underprivileged neighborhoods to access the same quality education as those living in wealthier neighborhoods.

Furthermore, it is argued that a voucher system will ensure that each child receives an education that is "reasonably close to the wishes of the families receiving the education," which is one of the stipulations for the role of government suggested above by Paul Brink. Besides, as is argued by a number of the contributors, the decision as to where a child receives an education should be made by the parents, not by any level of government.

But legitimate concerns have been raised about school voucher systems, the most notable being that its wholesale adoption could harm the current public school system in ways that have a perverse effect on the poorer families meant to benefit from the voucher system. For example, if students flock to private schools because of the availability of vouchers, public schools will lose the funding that states typically provide as a fixed amount per student.

I have in fact raised an oft-neglected concern that parents sending their children to an increasing number of private schools could lead to a form of tribalism, where students only engage with their "own kind."[3] To address that problem, I proposed that schools be allowed to receive such income from vouchers only if they agree to have their students participate in forums in which students from a diversity of neighborhood schools (public or private) engage each other in periodic conversations about their respective views on important societal

---

[3] Harold Heie, "Values in Public Education: Dialogue within Diversity," *Christian Scholar's Review*, 22, no. 2 (December 1992): 131–43.

issues, since this will make a strong contribution to the common good and avoid the temptation toward tribalism.

Another concern about vouchers that has been raised by some faith-based schools is a fear that receiving governmental funding, even if only indirectly through the parents of their children, could eventually lead to governmental interference in the education provided by the faith-based school.

Finally, there is a concern about "giving too much freedom of choice to parents." Consider the hypothetical case of a number of parents getting together to pool all their vouchers to start a new school that is segregated (African Americans, Asian Americans, and Latinos need not apply). Starting such a school would clearly violate the federal Civil Rights Act of 1964, which should ameliorate this concern.

Therefore, parents should not have the freedom to use voucher funds to start schools that clearly violate local, state, or federal laws. It is also my view that parents should not be allowed to start schools that provide a narrowly defined education that does not adequately lay the foundation for the follow-up education needed for responsible citizenship. Government needs to insure that that all students meet minimal standards for curriculum coverage and student achievement (more about that later).

Because I believe that parents should make the choice about who should educate their child, I am inclined to favor some type of voucher system for K–12 education, provided the details can be designed to overcome the concerns expressed above. But much more conversation is needed.

Should the distinction between "Public Schools" and "Private" Schools Be Maintained?

The tradition of providing free, compulsory public education for all

K–12 students in the United States has a venerable history in this country, starting shortly after the American Revolution, and expanding in the nineteenth century under the leadership of Horace Mann and Booker T. Washington.

In that light, Paul Brink is radical when he calls into question the long-standing distinction between public and private schools, suggesting that we should "just talk about schools," adding that "as long as children can graduate satisfying some minimal standards, we can call it a school." He elaborates on the reason for his proposal in terms of a perceived need to broaden the meaning of "community," as follows.

Rather than thinking that government should educate children (an idea he finds to "rather strange"), Brink prefers to "think of 'communities' educating their children." But he then raises the prior question as to "how community is understood."

Traditionally, "community" has been understood geographically, in terms of the city or town in which one happens to live. But Brink suggests that "today, community is more complicated. When people think of the community most relevant to the education of their children, many think of things other than geography: their faith traditions, their ideological commitments, their vocational interests, their educational philosophies." And recalling his earlier assertion that "government's interest in education . . . is ensuring that all children receive an education of reasonably high quality, and *reasonably close to the wishes of the families receiving the education*" (italics mine), he considers it an "injustice" if the wishes of the families for the education of their children is not adequately taken into account.

Who Should Establish Educational Policies and Standards for Student Achievement?

Stephen Monsma proposes that "communities—whether based on

geography or interests and beliefs" should be "the proper locus for setting and monitoring educational policy." This would suggest that, as much as possible, local communities should establish their own educational policies and standards for student performance. But, does this preclude a role for the state, or even the federal government, in setting educational policies and standards? One of our readers, Austin D., answers "no."

Austin taught in the Teach for America program and now works as an "education entrepreneur," consulting on "innovation and educational policy." He asserts that "education is an issue where different levels of government are necessary to address certain challenges." As already mentioned, an obvious example from our recent history is federal legislation of the Civil Rights Act of 1964, which made school segregation illegal. Local school districts could no longer segregate schools, and states that had supported practices of student segregation had to comply with the new federal law.

Austin cites a less clear-cut example from his home state of Texas. He says that "as evidenced by the history of decisions made about curriculum by the [Texas] State Board of Education, the state is very concerned with controlling the 'messages' education sends" adding that state officials have chosen "to emphasize certain ideas about the origins of humanity, [and] the reasons for the Civil War." He further notes that "it is in the state's interest to insure that the educators teaching their students are, to the extent that they can control it, 'in line' with those messages."

When does the federal government need to intervene into educational policies established by the state? I believe that judgment must be made on a case-by case basis, and opinions will differ about what judgment should be made. It eventually became clear, after too long a lapse of time, that state educational policies that denied equality of civil rights to African Americans, had to be overturned by the federal government, in light of its violation of the U.S. Constitution. No such violation is evident relative to questions about the origins of humanity.

Similarly, there may be cases when educational policies established by local school districts need to be overturned by the legislature or judiciary because they violate the state laws or the terms of a state constitution.

My point here is only this: even though the contributors and I believe local communities are typically the best locus for decisions about educational policies and standards, that does not mean we believe local communities should be given the right to "do as they please." In general, I would argue that the freedom of each "lower body" needs to be circumscribed by constraints established by the "next higher body."

Who Should Set and Monitor Standards for Teacher Certification?

Eric Teetsel considers his wife to be a "brilliant, talented and credentialed educator." He and his family, who now live in Washington, DC, hope to return to Kansas someday. "Yet, when we arrive, my wife will not be allowed to teach math or journalism in Kansas' public schools. State regulations require her to receive a Kansas-specific credential, which would require her to take a semester worth of coursework." This vignette reminds me of the time I heard someone lament the fact that Einstein would not have been able to teach high school physics in his home state of New Jersey.

As these stories reveal, standards for certifying K–12 teachers are set by the various states. Although clusters of states sometimes work together relative to certification expectations, there is no strong reciprocity in that a teacher has to apply for a license in a given state and meet that state's criteria. One of our readers, Travis, who is an "underemployed educator," longs for a "national credential that all states would have to recognize," which he believes "would provide a greater diversity of teachers, and thus effective teaching methods."

Austin D. explains why states want to have their own teacher certification, saying "native regulations and expectations ensure that incoming teachers meet the particular needs and goals of that particular state's education system." This could be a possible aspect of "controlling the message" noted above. He also adds that the reluctance of some states to enter reciprocity agreements is because "differing states could have different certification standards, making reciprocity unfair for states forced to hire lowly-qualified teachers from other states." Some have even suggested that states want their own certification requirements to "protect" the graduates of the education programs from their colleges and universities from a deluge of out-of-state applicants. Nevertheless, Austin agrees somewhat with Travis in suggesting that "federal policies establishing minimum requirements for teacher certification would be helpful."

What Is an Appropriate Balance between the "Freedom to Innovate" and Appropriate "Constraints" on Such Freedom?

Eric Teetsel suggests that "vouchers are a good start," because they provide parents with "choice," but he believes we should focus on "educational entrepreneurship," noting research has demonstrated that to be "the key to improvement."

Teetsel asks us to "imagine if the landscape of American education featured thousands of localized laboratories of innovation competing for the best practices for solving the many challenges we face," adding that "states and local communities could adopt and adapt programs according to their specific needs. Parents would be able to choose the most appropriate pathway for their child." His punch line is that "in education, as in everything, the freer we are the better we are."

Teetsel suggests that teacher unions are the primary obstacles to his vision for localized innovation because "*unions exist to serve teachers, not to serve students.*" He lays at the feet of teacher unions "the inability of school leaders to hire good teachers and fire bad ones, rigid policies regarding classroom time, and the ballooning costs of salaries, benefits and pensions."

Based on his experience as an "educational innovator," Austin D. calls into question the extent to which "freedom to innovate" should be limitless. He asserts that "education . . . requires a mix of openness and regulation to create the environment for innovation to happen," adding that "we must examine each opportunity on a case by case basis."

As a case in point, Austin refers to the federal program for promoting Common Core standards, a program that a large majority of the states have approved for setting student-learning standards in English language arts and mathematics. He suggests that "having a 'common language' about student learning for states . . . is highly advantageous for innovation" because without it, companies that produce content for classrooms would have to re-create their products "in 50 different ways to meet the needs of . . . 'customers.' This environment creates inefficiencies that inhibit the ability of entrepreneurs to scale their companies as they become overloaded with the amount of content they need to create." In this case, Austin says, "federal leadership would help to drive innovation."

Some of our contributors also disagree, directly or indirectly, with Eric Teetsel's low view of the role of teachers unions. To be sure, all the potential abuses that he points to have occurred. But, if it weren't for teachers unions, who would express a strong voice in opposition to the appalling pay scales for teachers that are still operative in many local school districts? As Amy Black asks, who would speak out against "overly bloated administrations wasting precious resources" rather than saving dollars for "the classroom, and investing in teachers, aides, and materials"? Who would speak out against "bureaucratic red tape," a problem noted by Austin D.? Who would speak out, asks Amy Black, against "the dangers of over-reliance on standardized tests to measure success"?

My punch line is that, whereas I am a firm believer in the ideal of "freedom," freedom "without boundaries" too easily deteriorates into license. I personally affirm that "in education, as in everything, we need to strike a balance between freedom and constraints on that freedom that will insure its responsible use."[4] To be sure, there will be much disagreement as to the exact nature of the needed constraints and the proper balance between "freedom" and "constraints on that freedom." Therefore, much more conversation is needed.

---

[4] The ideal of "freedom within bounds" is an integrative theme that has informed my thinking for many years. I even believe this ideal applies to my former teaching discipline of mathematics, as I argue in an essay titled "Mathematics: Freedom within Bounds" in Harold Heie and David L. Wolfe, ed., *The Reality of Christian Learning: Strategies for Faith-Discipline Integration* (Grand Rapids: Eerdmans, 1987), 206–230. Particularly pertinent to our present conversation is the epigraph to my essay, written by Michael Oakeshott: "Art and conduct, science, philosophy and history, these are not modes of thought defined by rules, they exist only in personal explorations of territories of which only the boundaries are subject to definition."

Gun Control

Common Ground

The United States Has a Severe Gun Violence Problem

Stephen Monsma asserts that "the numbers of gun deaths in the United States are appalling and should be the source of distress and alarm for everyone, and surely for every Christian who believes in the sanctity of God-created human life." He notes that in 2009, there were "some 83 gun-related deaths every day." The comparative data is more alarming: "for the most recent year I could find statistics, the United States had 14.4 gun-related homicides or suicides per 100,000 persons. The comparable figures for Canada was 4.4 deaths, for Germany 1.4 deaths, for England and Wales 0.4 deaths, and for Japan 0.06 deaths."

The Gun Problem Is a Cultural Problem with Deep Roots

These exact words from Amy Black are seconded by Eric Teetsel when he asserts that "ultimately, violence is a symptom of a cultural problem that goes much deeper than the mere availability of certain weapons." In that light, he proposes that "an effective approach to solving America's problem with violence would focus on the underlying causes, such as mental illness and psychological disorder, the breakdown of the traditional family and poverty."

One of our readers, Nathan Berkeley, adds his voice: "America's problems with gun violence . . . are problems rooted in other deeply harmful social problems. The guns are the medium by which other social (and/or spiritual) pathologies express themselves."

Amy Black notes that "there are no simple solutions" because of the deep-rooted, multiple causes of gun violence. But David Gushee points us to a possible place to start by distinguishing between what is "not new" and what is "new." In his own words:

> Sin is not new. Broken relationships are not new. Bad jobs are not new. Depression is not new. Hatred of the "other" is not new. Suicidal self-loathing is not new. Outbursts of anger are not new. But what does seem to be new, and unique to US culture, is the *ready availability of mass killing devices* in the hands of just about anyone who might ever feel like killing someone. (italics mine)

This observation suggests that the place to start in addressing gun violence is addressing the problem of the "ready availability of mass killing devices."

Commonsense Restrictions on the Availability and Use of Guns Need To Be Enacted

Eric Teetsel speaks for the contributors when he asserts that "putting aside extremists on both sides of the debate, sensible gun laws are uncontroversial," adding that "few would question the relatively minor inconvenience" of some of these restrictions.[1] A composite of such "sensible" restrictions proposed by the contributors follows.

- Ban the sale of large magazines of ammunition
- Require that all guns be sold with a trigger lock that needs a key or combination to unlock
- Require background checks, waiting periods and proper licensing for everyone purchasing a firearm, including those sold privately and at gun shows
- Require all gun purchasers to take a gun use and safety course and to present a certificate that they had taken such a course from an approved source before being able to purchase a firearm
- Reinstate the ban on the sale of assault weapons to civilians that was allowed to expire in 2004

Stephen Monsma proposes adding another restriction to "require that all privately-owned firearms must be kept in some sort of a locked storage drawer or cabinet." However, Amy Black would not want such a provision "written into law" although she agrees that it would "send a positive message about gun safety." Black says she is "uncomfortable about what it implies about the reach of government into private homes."

Questions for Further Conversation

Is the Deepest Cultural Problem a Flawed Understanding of "Individual Rights?"

The deep-rooted cultural causes of violence noted above (e.g., broken relationships, hatred) may not dig deep enough. Paul Brink suggests

---

[1] Lisa Sharon Harper did not post on this topic.

that the deepest problem may be "the American preoccupation with (and misunderstanding of) individual rights." He elaborates as follows: "An 'unrestricted right to gun ownership' is not a right. In fact, any 'unrestricted right' is not a right. For rights to be genuine, for rights to be effective, for rights to be humane, *for rights to be rights,* they must be placed into social and political contexts—and that means regulation."

Brink adds that "from a Christian perspective, this argument depends on a high view of human dignity . . . [that] will *pair rights with responsibilities,* individual freedoms with the obligation to ensure that the freedom of others will be respected" (italics mine).

Brink's view of the necessity to pair rights with obligations echoes my claim from the chapter on K–12 education that "freedom without boundaries too easily deteriorates into license" and that "in everything we need to strike a balance between freedom and constraints on that freedom that will insure its responsible use."

Interestingly, this focus on wedding freedom with responsibility comports well with the experience of Eric Teetsel, who recently took a hunter safety course as a birthday present to his father so that he "could some day join him" on regular hunting trips. Teetsel described this class as follows: "The instructors, all retired military, taught me to respect firearms and the culture of hunting. They endowed me with a sense of tremendous responsibility that comes with handling a rifle or shotgun." I wonder if these instructors were members of the NRA, which leads to my next question.

What Is the Proper Role of the NRA?

Amy Black reminds us of the motto of the National Rifle Association that was inscribed on its headquarters building in 1957: "Firearms Safety Education, Marksmanship Training, Shooting for Recreation."

I find no reason to object to this motto, and I find no evidence from their postings that any of the contributors would object to this motto. In fact, it fits marvelously with the goals of the instructors in Eric Teetsel's hunter safety course.

What has gone wrong since this motto was inscribed in 1957? Amy Black observes that "the NRA has moved quite some distance from its original purpose," noting that "NRA lobbyists now battle any and all legislative restrictions on guns and bullets, no matter how reasonable they may appear."

Paul Brink observes that the NRA often uses "slippery slope" arguments, "suggesting that waiting periods and trigger locks will somehow lead inexorably to government agents seizing hunting rifles" and suggests that such arguments "aren't helpful." That is putting it mildly. I personally find it incomprehensible that anyone could believe this particular slippery slope argument.

So, if the NRA has indeed strayed from its original purpose, what can now be done? The answer may lie with the NRA membership. Consider, for example, the fact that after the gun massacre in Newtown, Connecticut, a survey revealed that 74 percent of NRA members supported a requirement for background checks for the sale of guns in secondary markets, such as gun shows.[2] This statistic surfaced about the same time that an NRA executive adamantly refused to even consider the possibility of any of the commonsense restrictions on guns and bullets like those proposed above. It makes one wonder what influence, if any, the NRA membership has on the positions taken by the NRA leadership and adds credence to the claim that the NRA is more beholden to gun manufacturers than to its members. This suggests it is time for the NRA members who

---

[2] A first draft of this chapter was completed three days before the Connecticut massacre.

disagree with the intransigence of the NRA leadership to speak up and say "enough is enough"; it is time to return to the original purpose of the organization.

Stephen Monsma even suggests that gun owners who are not currently members of the NRA and who disagree with the NRA leadership should "join the NRA and urge a more responsible, balanced position on its leadership."

What Does the Second Amendment Say?

This question can best be addressed by those with expertise in constitutional law. However, a number of our contributors posted some valuable insights.

The Second Amendment says, "A well regulated militia, being necessary to the security of a free state, the right of the people to keep and bear Arms, shall not be infringed." It is important to note the historical context for this amendment. As pointed out by David Gushee, "the Second Amendment was written at a time when the greatest fear was the tyranny of centralized power over the individual citizen or the local community."

Eric Teetsel's similar take is that "the right to gun ownership was included among the ten freedoms made explicit in the Bill of Rights because these early Americans were sensitive to future encroachments on liberty that might necessitate acts of self-defense."

But it appears to be a stretch to go from this historical understanding to the call for an unrestricted right to gun ownership. As Paul Brink says, "the idea that an 'unrestricted right to gun ownership' must be maintained as a protection against government power sounds just a little over the top to contemporary ears, especially when America's closest friends and allies place significant restrictions on gun ownership and so far have managed to avoid the descent into tyranny."

David Gushee suggests that when the Second Amendment was adopted, the greatest fear was the tyranny of centralized power, but that "today our greatest fear surely must be the tyranny of individual gun violence over all of us." If that assessment is accurate, what are the implications for our contemporary understanding of the Second Amendment?

Why Is It Likely that any Proposed Gun Control Legislation Will Be Dead on Arrival in Congress?

David Gushee has had his fill with politicians who speak "mournfully" after each gun massacre but then do absolutely nothing to reduce the possibility of the next massacre. Reflecting on the responses of politicians to the summer 2012 gun massacres in Aurora, Colorado, and at a Sikh temple in Wisconsin, Gushee says:

> All the response we seem to get from our politicians is an ineffectual spray of mournful words. None are ready, willing or able to diagnose the deeper sources of our gun-massacre culture or to offer social or policy solutions. The meaninglessness of priestly words of comfort from political leaders responsible for solving public problems has by now moved to the level of the obscene. We should declare a national moratorium on such mournful words from politicians, who should instead be held accountable for developing a bipartisan plan to stop the mayhem.

Why is the mourning after each gun massacre followed by legislative inaction? It appears that too many politicians fear that if they stand up to the NRA and the gun lobbyists, who have enormous financial resources, they will not get elected or re-elected. Although there is some data to support that concern, some pundits have recently observed that this has not always been the outcome of standing up to the NRA. In any case, David Gushee's exhortation needs to be heard: "We need politicians with the courage to face down the ridiculous and in fact lethal demands of the gun lobby."

I present the failure of politicians to enact commonsense gun control legislation as Exhibit A in support of my contention that the primary problem with our broken political system is that the focus is placed on getting elected, rather than where the focus should be: governing in a way that promotes the common good.

What Can Be Done To Address the Deep-Rooted Cultural Causes of Gun Violence?

The agreement among the contributors that our gun violence problem has multiple causes is supported by the report on the Newtown, Connecticut, massacre committed by Adam Lanza. The report tentatively concludes that Lanza's "unique combination of mental illness, family brokenness, and immersion in gun culture led him to plot . . . one of the most shocking killing sprees in American history."[3] The existence of such multiple causes of gun violence call for multiple strategies to address this problem.

Starting with a global strategy, Stephen Monsma asserts that— beyond the commonsense restrictions on the purchase and use of guns that he and other contributors have proposed—what is "more important" is the need for "a change in cultural values and beliefs." For those who see this as wishful thinking, Monsma points to two cultural examples where we have seen such changes in recent years:

---

[3] Aaron Belz, "Thoughts on the Newtown Massacre," *Capital Commentary*, December 21, 2012.

"Smoking has changed from being glamorous and sexy to being just plain stupid." And, "the ideal woman has morphed from being weak and dependent to being strong, accomplished and self-reliant."

Monsma argues that "a similar cultural change is needed in the case of guns." He observes that "today, our society relates gun ownership and gun knowledgeableness with being manly, self-reliant and even sexy" (as demonstrated by "a recent internet ad for a firearm that describes it as 'The rifle that brings out the West in you'"). Monsma says "that needs to change so that guns are seen as being dangerous and with the potential for antisocial uses."

Many others besides politicians need to contribute if this cultural change is to take place. The entertainment industry needs to end its glamorization of violence, both in its films and TV shows and in its video games, which seem to take violence to a new level. Stephen Monsma asserts that, in sharp contrast to present practice:

> the entertainment industry could help by portraying the harm to which guns can lead, and not as the quick solution to problems. The news casts and news commentators can add their voice. Statistics on gun deaths and their causes should be the object of more scholarly studies . . . that the media could then cover and highlight. Doctors who work in trauma centers and daily observe the damage guns do need to find their voice. Pastors need to speak out. Right-to-life groups need to speak out against needless gun deaths as they do against deaths by abortion. And all of us citizens can join advocacy organizations urging action designed to curb gun violence.

David Gushee notes steps that can be taken in our homes, suggesting that "we need to raise our children who will become adults who know how to control themselves when faced with intoxicants, broken relationships, problems with parents, sexual jealousy, depression, loneliness, and really bad bosses."

I believe more "preventative" steps also need to be taken. Funding for mental health services need to be increased, not cut. Legislation is needed that allows for the identification and treatment of those needing psychological help before their mental illness drives them to horrific gun violence.

What I found so discouraging in the aftermath of the Connecticut massacre was to hear politicians and other persons in leadership positions in society acknowledge the multiple causes of gun violence, but then proceed to preclude addressing one or more of these causes. For example, I heard an NRA leader suggest that there are multiple causes for gun violence, emphasizing the need for improved mental health services (so far, so good), but then refuse to even entertain the possibility that outlawing the sale of assault weapons and large magazines of ammunition could also be of some help. For me, this points to the need for an approach to the problem of gun violence that seeks for a balance between various strategies, none of which are sufficient when standing alone.

I close this section by noting that all the contributors propose that Christians bear a special responsibility to address the deep-rooted causes of gun violence because of Christian teachings about "the sanctity of human life." As David Gushee puts it, "life is sacred," and therefore, "we need higher value to be placed on human life."

Eric Teetsel adds the following exhortation to all those who profess commitment to the Christian faith: "Christians must continue to spread our message of life and love, knowing that ultimately the Gospel is the only impediment to violence and sin."

Abortion

Common Ground

Elective Abortion-on-Demand Ought to Be Prohibited by Public Policy

Based on the biblical teachings that "human life is a gift from God" and that "all humankind bears God's image and is sacred," Amy Black asserts that "we should value human life and seek to protect it from conception until natural death." Therefore, she argues that we should "move . . . away from abortion-on-demand."

Similarly, David Gushee asserts that "elective abortion is the volitional destruction of human life at its earliest stages." None of the contributors argue in favor of abortion-on-demand.

Stephen Monsma makes clear that the basis for prohibiting abortion-on-demand is a value commitment, a matter of "determining the value that should be attached to the human life that abortion ends." Therefore, speaking for himself and many other Christians, he says that "we do not believe almost all abortions should be illegal simply because we believe they are wrong and against God's will," because "there are many other things we believe are wrong and against God's will—such as taking God's name in vain, fornication and gossiping—that we do not believe should be illegal." Rather, he says, "what is different about abortion is that it involves taking another human life and our faith causes us to value human life very highly."

So, the foundational value for the contributors is the "value of human life." Of course, this raises the question as to whether an embryo or a fetus can be considered to be "human life." This question is much debated. As Amy Black points out, "the two sides [pro-life and pro-choice] fundamentally disagree about the status of the embryo and the fetus." How can that disagreement be navigated?

Both Stephen Monsma and David Gushee address this question by appealing to recent scientific findings. Monsma suggests that "modern science has not been kind to the prochoice position," elaborating by saying that "as science has learned more about fetal development, it has pushed back to the very early stages of pregnancy the presence of a very small, but complete human being—to within the first seven weeks." Gushee suggests that "contemporary ultrasound technology . . . has made it harder to deny the humanity of the developing child."

This appeal to recent scientific findings may still not be convincing to someone who believes that the fetus is not "human life" before birth. My response to that person is that even at the earliest stages of development, the fetus is at least "nascent human life," and, as such, is of value and should be protected unless some overriding value can be appealed to, which leads to the next area of common ground.

Public Policy Should Allow for Abortion in Certain Tragic Situations

None of the contributors argue for public policy that would ban all abortions. For example, at the same time Amy Black affirms that she would "support public policy that that moves toward an end goal of banning elective abortion," she allows for "exceptions for cases of rape, incest, and threat to the health of the mother."

To get at the deeper question of why exceptions are called for in these three cases, consider the hypothetical example of my wife and I being faced with the exceptional case noted above when the life of the mother is threatened by a continuing pregnancy. If my wife were pregnant and medical experts told us she was very likely to die if her pregnancy were not terminated, that, in my estimation, would be an adequate justification for choosing an abortion because my wife has established loving personal relationships the fetus has not established. Therefore, we would be sacrificing one value (the life of the fetus) for what we judged to be a higher value (the life of my wife). Although the contributors do not delineate possible "exceptions" beyond the three noted above, my hypothetical example illustrates my belief that an exception may be given consideration (in concrete cases, not in abstract discussions around a seminar table) when circumstances are such that the people involved reach the painful judgment that the value of the form of life of the fetus is overridden by a higher value, and one chooses for the higher value.

Steps Should Be Taken to Reduce the Number of Abortions

As heated as the debate on abortion is, I have heard people on both sides of this issue agree that concrete steps should be taken to reduce the number of abortions. My contributors agree. For example, Amy Black asserts that "almost everyone agrees that abortion is a tragic decision, so we can at least work together to reduce the number of abortions," adding that "we can also find common cause supporting meaningful restrictions on abortion designed to protect women's health."

Amy Black and Eric Teetsel point us to the importance of helping women who experience unwanted pregnancies. Given the call for Christians to "give particular care to the poor and vulnerable" (see Matthew 25), Black reminds Christians that "women facing unwanted pregnancies and the lives growing inside of them are among the most vulnerable ones God call us to love and serve."

Citing the work of "Care Net, a national network of 1,100 crisis pregnancy centers," Teetsel notes that "crisis pregnancy centers offer women in need a heaping dose of compassion and provision." He adds that the crisis centers "help to take the fear out of an unanticipated pregnancy, allowing women to make an informed clear-headed choice about what to do next. And, when given such a choice, the vast majority choose life." He concludes with an exhortation to "find a crisis pregnancy center near you. Donate your time, resources and money to their work. Spread the word. Advocate the building of new clinics that can serve even more women."

Reader Nathan Berkeley points us to other "partial and incomplete legal protections for the unborn." Included in his list are laws that define abortion clinics as full-fledged medical clinics and subject them to more stringent regulations, laws that require women considering abortion to have an ultrasound as an attempt to better inform them about the reality of the fetus, and laws that prohibit abortion based on gender discrimination or particular disabilities of an unborn child.

Another means to reduce the number of abortions is to better facilitate adoption opportunities and procedures. In the journal *Perspectives,* Calvin College history professor James Bratt quotes David Frum, a former speechwriter to President George W. Bush, as having said the following just a week before the 2012 elections: "as a general rule, societies that do the most to support mothers and child-bearing have the fewest abortions. Societies that do the least to support mothers and child-bearing have more abortions." Commenting on Frum's observation, Bratt asserts that "such support begins with health care and economic viability."[1] This suggests that steps need to be taken to address the root cause of poverty that leads some women to choose abortion because they cannot envision the possibility of covering the expenses of raising a child.

Opponents of Abortion-on-Demand Should Advocate for Incremental Steps in the Direction of Overturning Roe v. Wade

For those hoping to see *Roe v. Wade* overturned, David Gushee recommends an incremental approach. In his own words, "changes in abortion law need to be incremental, including a relatively broad range of exceptions (rape, incest, threat to the life of the mother) for there to be any hope of public acceptance of an overturn of *Roe v. Wade*."

Amy Black thinks it prudent to begin with an incremental approach, explaining that she "support[s] public policy that moves toward the end goal of banning elective abortion with exceptions for cases of rape, incest, and threat to the life of the mother."

Paul Brink also supports an incremental approach, saying that "while I personally find many of the pro-life arguments to be persuasive, I think it spectacularly unwise to seek nothing less than a full abortion ban," adding that "in the America in which I live today, there are simply too many people who disagree . . . and so I have to accept that for the time being, any legal protections for unborn children that we might advance politically will be partial and incomplete."

Opponents of Abortion-on-Demand Should Take a Consistent and Comprehensive Pro-Life Position

David Gushee asserts that "Christian opposition to abortion is best understood as part of a holistic Christian ethic of the sacredness of human life from womb to tomb."

---

[1] James Bratt, "An Obsolete Political Faith," *Perspectives*, November 2012, 5.

Steve Monsma concurs, saying that "our position on abortion should be only one way in which the high value we place on human life shows itself." He also implies that other "prolife issues" are "limiting the easy availability of guns, feeding the hungry, providing medical care for the aged and disabled" and not quickly "resorting to military action."

Amy Black echoes Monsma's broad view of pro-life issues when, in elaborating on her assertion that "a pro-life commitment extends beyond the abortion issue," she bemoans the fact that "we often turn a blind eye to the pain and suffering of children and adults all around us, tacitly accepting poverty, hunger, disease, discrimination, racism, and other evils that devalue God's image-bearers."

Questions for Further Conversation

How Should People Taking a Pro-Life Position Engage in Public Conversations with Those Who Disagree with Them?

The abortion debate appears to be intractable. While there may be enough fault to go around, part of the problem on the pro-life side, as pointed out by Amy Black, may be that "a few vocal activists are shrill and insensitive." Black asserts that "most of those in the pro-life movement are warm-hearted, caring people with deep concern for the women and men affected by unplanned pregnancy," but, unfortunately, the shrill voices are often the only voices that gain a hearing.

Another problem that inhibits genuine, respectful conversation on this volatile issue, according to Stephen Monsma, is the perception that religious people taking a pro-life position are "seeking to impose their religious beliefs on all of society."

Monsma also points out that a pro-life position could gain a better hearing if it were expressed as a consistent and comprehensive ethic. In his own words, "I am convinced that to the extent we who are prolife Christians link our prolife position on abortion to a heartfelt, active commitment to the sanctity of human life in other settings, our position on abortion will gain increased respect and a renewed, serious hearing."

How can we get beyond this impasse? Paul Brink, in response to reader Nathan Berkeley, points us in a promising direction when he suggests that those proposing regulations regarding abortion "can appeal to how these regulations fit into larger moral frameworks— even perhaps moral frameworks that their opponents may be able to affirm." (Or, at a minimum, I would suggest, "be able to understand").

One possibility for this larger moral framework is to focus on "value commitments," which we all have. In the words of Stephen Monsma, Christians need to make a case based on the indisputable facts of fetal development, combined with *"the high value our faith places on human life"* (italics mine). He adds that "our faith tells us what value to place on human life and this is where we disagree with our prochoice fellow citizens." In that case, Monsma asserts, pro-choice advocates would "need to argue their case on the basis that they disagree with us on *the value we attach to pre-birth human life"* (italics mine).

If the debate takes place at this foundational level of "value commitments," those in the pro-choice movement will surely point to the high value that they place on a "woman's right to choose." Although the contributors do not directly address that particular value commitment, my view is as follows.

As I have suggested elsewhere in this volume, I believe in the freedom to choose, albeit within boundaries. In the case of abortion, the "boundary question" is how to navigate a conflict between the "value of pre-birth human life" and the value of a "woman's right to choose." My belief is that if faced with such an apparently irreconcilable conflict, I must choose in favor of the "value of pre-birth human life," except in exceptional cases of rape, incest, and threat to the life of the mother.

Note that when the debate takes place at the level of foundational value commitments, the reasons given by those on both sides of the issue are what David Gushee calls "public reasons," expressed in terms of each person's understanding of "human values" that we can share because of our common humanity, whatever our religious or secular world-view commitments. It is not a matter of any one particular religious or secular group trying to impose its particular beliefs on all of society.

How Should Public Policy Protect the Religious Freedom of Doctors and Faith-Based Hospitals Who Object to Any or All Forms of Abortion on Religious Grounds?

This question continues the conversation begun in the conversation on religious freedom. I believe it is fair to surmise from my report on that conversation that most of our contributors, if not all, would argue for "appropriate exemptions" to laws prescribing abortion provisions for doctors and faith-based hospitals who object to such provisions on religious grounds.

Does Our Society Depend on Abortion to Underwrite its Sexual and Romantic Practices?

David Gushee raises this provocative question when he boldly asserts that "the United States, like much of the rest of the 'advanced' world, is a society that depends on abortion as to underwrite its sexual and romantic practices."

Gushee elaborates by stating that "overturning earlier strictures confining sex to marriage has increased the expectation that people will have sex outside of marriage, and thus has increased women's vulnerability to unwanted pregnancies," which too often leads to decisions for abortion. He makes the dire prediction that "until we learn to break our social dependence on abortion, there will always be mass elective abortion in the United States, no matter who is elected or what the law says."

The Role
of Government

Common Ground

Government Is a God-Established Institution to Promote Justice and the Common Good in Society

The above words from Stephen Monsma's posting echo the fourth of the five "Basic Christian Principles for Politics and Public Policy," summarized in the introductory chapter, which all the contributors agreed to prior to our Alternative Political Conversation. As will soon be seen, however, our contributors do not agree on the meaning of "justice" or the proper role of government in promoting the common good.[1]

Human Sinfulness Is a Reality

As Stephen Monsma observes, "a Christian perspective on public policy, as all of us who are writing these [web postings] agree, includes . . . human beings' fallen, sinful nature." In Amy Black's words, "the

---

[1] Lisa Sharon Harper did not post on this topic. For her views on the role of government, see the chapter titled "Liberty and Justice: On the Role of Government," in Lisa Sharon Harper & D. C. Innes, *Left, Right and Christ: Evangelical Faith in Politics* (Boise, Idaho: Russell Media, 2011).

reality of life in a fallen and broken world is that everything is tainted by sin."

As stated in the "Basic Christian Principles for Politics and Public Policy," this reality does not diminish the "god-given worth or dignity" that humans have as a result of being "created as God's image bearers and the crowning achievement of His creation." But it does mean that whereas "governments and their public policies can bring about good in society, they will always be subject to flaws and failures." It will soon become apparent that our contributors disagree as to how government should guard against—or at least minimize—the destructive effects of such flaws and failures.

Government and Nongovernmental Institutions of Civil Society, such as Families, Schools, Churches, Businesses, and Voluntary Organizations, All Have Roles to Play in a Flourishing Society

In commenting on SNAP (Supplemental Nutrition Assistance Program), Eric Teetsel asserts that "feeding hungry people is a really good thing," since "it's one of the essential elements of a Christian life." But, he continues, "the critical question for those of us concerned with helping these people is how to lift them out of poverty." Teetsel believes "there exist biblically sound roles for government, morality, the family, free enterprise, and civil society to work together. But, each must remain committed to its appropriate sphere."

Paul Brink states that he "can strongly affirm [Teetsel's] . . . emphasis on the distinct roles of state and church. The state cannot take upon itself the task of the church—it does not 'speak to soul' in the way that the church does. Similarly, when the church takes upon itself the responsibilities of the state, all sorts of distortions and problems appear."

Questions remain as to the relationships between the responsibilities of government and the responsibilities of the nongovernmental institutions of civil society.

Questions for Further Conversation
How "Big" Should Government Be?

Consider with me, in order, what my contributors had to say about the elements of a minimalist (baseline) role for government, perceived problems with the minimalist view, elements of an expanded role for government, and potential problems with an expanded view.

What Is a Minimalist Role for Government?

David Gushee succinctly describes "the baseline role of government" as "providing law and order services domestically and security services internationally," adding that these two elements are "what most everyone understands to be part of what even a minimalist government needs to do."

Amy Black concurs with Gushee that, domestically, "government . . . maintains the 'rule of law' to create clear boundaries for how people can live and work together peacefully." But, she adds that government also has the "essential function" of providing "'public goods'—those basic goods and services that are beneficial to many people, meet significant needs, and are available to everyone equally." (The Interstate Highway System and National Parks come to my mind under this function).

Black then adds a third essential function: "Government helps sustain private institutions such as schools, churches, and families that are essential partners for building and maintaining a robust society." This third essential function comports with the third area of common ground noted above.

Eric Teetsel's agreement with Black on this third essential function is seen in his statement that "the role of government is to protect the freedom of individuals, churches and local communities to go about their tasks." However, he adds that "the government is ordained with the role of maintaining peace and justice, enabling us to live together in relative harmony."

Note that Teetsel's proposal that government has the role of "maintaining peace" fits well with the proposals from both Gushee and Black. However, he also says that the role of government includes "maintaining justice," possibly adding a new dimension that could take us beyond a "minimalist" view of government, depending on how the meaning of "justice" is defined. (More about that later).

There is agreement among the contributors, however, that a "minimalist" government maintains the law and order necessary to enable citizens to live in peace and harmony, provides for appropriate "public goods," and enables the private institutions of civil society to effectively carry our their roles in building and maintaining a flourishing society.

Are There Any Problems with This Minimalist View of the Role of Government?
In commenting on federal food programs, Eric Teetsel says that "we will no longer require federal food programs when families are kept intact, a culture of hard work is reaffirmed, the free enterprise system is properly regulated to protect the vital role of entrepreneurs, and the other institutions of civil society (schools, local communities) take up their respective roles in the process of building up and sending our virtuous citizens." This suggests that a minimalist view of the role of government will suffice, at least relative to "feeding hungry people," if the free enterprise system and other institutions of civil society are adequately carrying out their responsibilities.

But other contributors question whether the problems facing our society can be adequately addressed without government playing more than the minimalist role noted above. For example, in response to one of our readers, Stephen Monsma asserts that "churches and individuals cannot be expected to meet all or most of the needs present in society." And Amy Black says that while "families, churches and other community institutions have essential roles in caring for the needy . . . these systems sometimes fail, and some problems and conditions are so deeply rooted in the structure of society that government is likely the last but best response to address them."

David Gushee is especially concerned about the failures of "capitalism" that he believes call for governmental intervention. While acknowledging that "modern capitalism has been the great driver of economic, technological, and cultural development in the modern world," Gushee suggests that "it became clear quite early in the career of industrial capitalism that it produced numerous losers as well as winners." He says the losers included:

> Workers (including women and children) abused by overlong hours and unsafe working conditions; mass urban workforces at the mercy of business owners and the business cycle; failed businesses and those who lost their jobs when they failed; communities harmed by environmental "externalities" of profit-hungry industries; villages and cities dominated by business monopolies; those who lacked skills or the good health to work.

In light of this history of industrial capitalism, Gushee adds that "much of the modern role of government is best understood as a response both to capitalism's failures and its most radical critics." Hence:

Government protects the environment because we know business on its own will fail to do so voluntarily. Government educates children (or requires that they be educated) and now protects children from being drawn prematurely into the workforce. Government (sometimes) regulates both the health and safety of workplaces and the activities of banks and investors, because we know that business on its own will not do so adequately . . . Government programs for the poor, the sick, the disabled, and the aged seek to provide income support to those unable to participate (any longer) in the workforce.

David Gushee's punch line is that "Christians who hold a realistic understanding of sin, together with an informed understanding of the history of modern capitalism, must reject the claim that that an unregulated capitalist business sector can be counted on both to pursue profit and to advance the common good."

Is There an Expanded View of Government that Adequately Addresses the Perceived Problems with a Minimalist View?

As already noted above, David Gushee has proposed that to address "capitalism's failures" in a way that promotes the common good, one must go beyond a minimalist view of the role of government to include regulations that protect the environment, that protect children and workers, that create boundaries for the activities of banks and investors, and that assist those who, through no fault of their own, do not fare well in a free-market economy.

A number of the contributors suggest that the necessary expanded activities of government (beyond the minimalist view), such as those suggested above, will contribute to the common good and can best be captured under the rubric of "doing justice." The concept of justice has been appealed to a number of times in our previous conversations, and it emerged again in this conversation. It is time to clarify the meaning of this multifaceted concept.

In the broadest sense, "doing justice" means "giving people their due," or "treating people fairly." This applies to individuals as well as groups of people. For example, as noted above, it calls for government to enable nongovernmental institutions to carry out their respective responsibilities—what some, like those associated with the Center for Public Justice (CPJ), have referred to as "structural pluralism." It also calls for government to provide a "level playing field" for those committed to a variety of religious or secular world views to express their respective views in public life—what CPJ refers to as "confessional pluralism."

When it comes to doing justice relative to individual persons or the engagement between two persons, justice has multiple dimensions. "Commutative justice" requires fairness in agreements and exchanges between private parties (e.g., contracts should be kept). "Procedural justice" defines the procedures and processes that must be fair if other dimensions of justice are to prevail (e.g., courts should be unbiased).

A third dimension is "distributive justice," which refers to a "fair" distribution of goods and rights among persons. Of course, the meaning of "fair" can be debated endlessly. At a minimum, the Bible clearly teaches that commitment to distributive justice calls Christians to be agents for a better distribution of goods and rights to the poor, the marginalized, and oppressed of the world (Matthew 25).

A fourth dimension is "retributive justice," sometimes called "corrective justice," which defines what is due to people when they have done wrong. Wrongdoers should receive an appropriate punishment. I happen to believe such punishment can be administered in ways that focus on restoration, not retribution. Therefore, I refer to this aspect as "restorative justice."[2]

With these various dimensions of justice as background, recall that Eric Teetsel proposed that it is the role of government to "maintain peace and justice." But from my reading of his elaboration on this proposal, it appears to me that Teetsel is focusing on the "retributive justice" dimension that deals with appropriate forms of punishment for those who have disrupted the peace, harmony, and order of society by violating the law. For example, he says that "ultimately justice is about the application of *power*," providing the following examples: "The lawyer who prosecuted D. C. sniper John Allen Muhammad, the judge who sentenced him to death, and the official who injected the lethal medication in his arm acted justly"; and "by distributing tickets to illegal parkers the state is administering justice."

To be sure, administering retributive justice is an important task for government as it carries out its minimalist role of maintaining law and order in society. But the expanded role for government suggested above is primarily informed by the "distributive justice" dimension.

In this volume, the "working definition" of distributive justice that I have been assuming is that proposed by Paul Brink in the chapter on the federal budget deficit: "justice requires that all members of society have the ability to participate in our common life." The ideal that Brink embraces, with which I concur, requires the expanded view of government pointed to above.

---

[2] The vision of the Restorative Justice movement does not preclude punishment. But it is broader in scope than just punishment. It focuses on meeting the needs of all persons affected by the breaking of a law, not just the offender, but also those who are victimized by the law-breaking, and the communities in which both the offender and the victims live. The ultimate goal is to restore harmonious relationships between all persons involved and promote the flourishing of all persons. For readers interested in learning more about the Restorative Justice movement, I recommend Howard Zehr, *Changing Lenses* (Scottdale, PA: Herald Press, 1990).

Are There Any Problems with This Expanded View of the Role of Government?

But there is surely potential for abuse in implementing an expanded view of government. The "darker forces in human nature" referred to by Stephen Monsma are not revealed only when selfishness and greed distort a properly functioning free market system. These darker forces also surface when an overbearing government completely stifles the freedom for individuals and groups of individuals to give responsible expression to their God-given creative abilities, both at home and in nations subject to dictatorial rule. This suggests a possible need for balance, which is the focus of my next question.

Is There a Need for Balance?

A number of the contributors point to the need for balance between the role of government and the roles of nongovernmental sectors of society. In commenting on the position of "traditional conservatives," Stephen Monsma notes that they "fear both an overly weak and an overly intrusive government" (adding that the "position adopted by the Romney-Ryan ticket is not traditional conservatism," but leans more toward "libertarianism").

Drawing on the thought of Reinhold Niebuhr, David Gushee suggests that "concentrations of power are intrinsically dangerous wherever they appear. Thus unchecked capitalism is dangerous. So is unchecked government. Unchecked owners are dangerous. But so are unchecked unions. Power corrupts. Great centers of power need to be checked by other great centers of power."

Amy Black suggests that we have learned through "centuries of trial and error" that "too little government leads to chaos and entrenched poverty; too much government control leads to fear and oppression," adding that "the key to good government is finding the *right balance* between too weak and too strong" (italics mine).

As an example, Black observes that "all modern democracies recognize the need for upholding both free markets and a regulatory
state; they differ over *how to balance these competing interests*" (italics
mine). She also urges us to keep "looking for the *right balance* of
individual and collective ways we can be agents of restoration and
help secure the common good" (italics mine).

Stephen Monsma notes that the search for the right balance is
not static; it is a dynamic process that calls for "thoughtful discussion of where government is working well and where it is not, where
government action is needed and where it is not" (a judgment with
which Amy Black concurs). And Monsma adds that in this dynamic
process "the standard for evaluating existing and proposed programs
ought not to be our own self-interest . . . justice and the common
good are the correct standards."

Amy Black also suggests that "properly-functioning governments
rely on mutual accountability. Governments and their citizens are
accountable to one another and all (whether they admit it or not) are
ultimately accountable to God." She concludes that "a good and effective government therefore creates a community of mutual accountability and responsibility where everyone gives and receives."

I would add that this quest for balance extends well beyond the
much-needed balance between governments and their citizens as
addressed by Black. A recurring theme throughout these twelve conversations has been the need for balance between competing views
on particular public policy issues. I will remind you of a number of
illustrative examples.

There is little hope for solving the federal budget deficit problem
unless a balance is struck between the need for cuts in expenditures
and the need for increased revenues.

Those debating the immigration issue must balance the call for improved border protection and punishment of those who have entered our country illegally with the pressing need to provide a viable pathway to citizenship for those undocumented workers who are making an enormous contribution to our economy and our country and whose families are being decimated by current immigration laws.

The seemingly intractable conflict between Israel and Palestine has no hope of a solution unless it is recognized that the only viable solution will need to treat both Israelis and Palestinians justly— enabling both peoples to flourish. As in all attempts to achieve a proper balance, either/or solutions will not work; both/and solutions are required.

In the debate on health care, it is not only a matter of providing health care for many who have been uninsured. That need must be balanced by the need to reduce the spiraling costs of health care.

The current debates regarding K–12 education need to strike a balance between the importance of providing "freedom for entrepreneurial innovation" and regulations that will prevent some expressions of such freedom from harming certain segments of our society.

In the gun control debate, the choice is not between either addressing the mental health and culture of violence problems that beset our nation or legislatively enacting some commonsense gun control measures. It has to be both.

I could go on. But by now you get my point.

If I am right about the need to seek a proper balance between competing views on most public policy issues, then that points to what I believe is the primary reason for the current gridlock in Washington. Those who are on the extremes on both sides of the aisle are essentially committed to the necessity of either/or solutions to our most pressing problems. It is "either my way or the highway," which leaves no room for seeking both/and solutions that reflect the best thinking on both sides of the aisle.

This suggests to me a greater need for what some pundits have called "governing from the middle," not being beholden to the extremists in either major party. Of course, this is much easier said than done since enormous amounts of money are expended on promoting the election of those with extreme views and thwarting the political aspirations of those who wish to engage in "principled compromise" with members of the other party to work toward balanced solutions to our most pressing societal problems.

To be sure, seeking the best balance between competing views on any public policy issue is no easy task. It is much easier to argue for either/or solutions that lend themselves to sixty-second soundbites or memorable bumper stickers. Those committed to finding the best balance between competing views will often disagree strongly about what the best balance is. Much further conversation will be needed regarding any given issue. That is why I believe my plea for respectful conversation among those who disagree with one another is vital for future political discourse.

What Is the Meaning of "Love"?

Paul Brink and Eric Teetsel have a fascinating exchange that brings to the surface a need to be clear about the meaning of "love," and its relationship to justice.

Whereas he agrees with Teetsel that "charity [is] . . . a primary responsibility of the church," Brink adds that "charity is not the only way we demonstrate love for neighbors . . . To love our neighbor is not only to extend him or her charity; it is also to see that justice is done for our neighbor." He concludes that "this means that we love our neighbors not only in church, but actually love them in the state as well."

In a response that is cleverly titled "The Warm Embrace of the Department of Motor Vehicles," Teetsel disagrees with Brink, arguing that "bureaucracies can't love."

Brink responds by asserting that "bureaucracies can love." He explains that "they demonstrate that love in ways that are appropriate to state bureaucracies: that is, in the administration of public justice. How we love our neighbors is multi-faceted: in church we love through our charity, in the state we love through justice."

How can one sort through this disagreement? Brink gives a hint when he concedes that "when I have waited in line at the DMV, or filled out tax returns, or received parking tickets, I can't say I have *felt* a lot of love in those moments" (italics mine).

My own view is that love is not most basically a feeling, although it can be accompanied by deep feelings. Love is most fundamentally an action. I decide to act in a certain way toward another person or group of persons. I believe I express my love for another person when I decide to act in a way that contributes to his or her well-being and ability to flourish. So, I don't expect any warm fuzzies from the clerk at the DMV. But when he or she helps me to renew my driver's license, she is contributing to my well-being and is thereby "loving me."

It is fitting that I close my contributions to this volume by reflecting on the meaning of love, for two reasons. First, I have come to believe that the essence of what it means for me to be a follower of Jesus is my aspiration to be obedient to the two great love commandments Jesus left as a summary of all his teachings: "You shall love the Lord your God with all your heart, and with all your soul, and with all your mind, and with all your strength . . . [and] you shall love your neighbor as yourself" (Mark 12:28–31).

Second, I come back full circle to my main motivation for writing this book, as started in the concluding paragraph in my introductory chapter. I believe that a deep expression of love for another person is to give that person a welcoming space to disagree on important issues and to then engage in respectful conversation about such disagreements, thereby opening up the potential for mutual learning. It is my hope and prayer that the twelve conversations reported on in this volume model my commitment to this ideal, as well as the shared commitment of the contributors.

CONTRIBUTOR REFLECTIONS

Modeling a More Excellent Way

Thoughts on Respectful Dialogue

AMY E. BLACK

Not long after Barack Obama's election in 2008, bumper stickers began to appear on cars that read "Pray for Obama" and included the Scripture reference "Psalm 109:8." At first glance, such stickers looked like a worthy Christian endeavor enjoining others to lift up the president in prayer. But anyone who checked the specific biblical passage would find these ominous words: "May his days be few; may another take his place of leadership." The verses that immediately follow offer even stronger curses, such as "may his children be fatherless and his wife a widow."

This bumper sticker is just one painful example of misuse of Scripture and the cruelty and disrespect that is all too common in contemporary politics. Christians are indeed called to pray for their leaders—whether they voted for them or not—but this biblical command is a serious matter, not an excuse for a cruel joke.

The Alternative Political Conversation was an excellent opportunity for evangelical Christians to model a different way to talk about politics, and I am glad I was able to participate. By assembling six contributors from across the ideological spectrum, the project offered readers the chance to read a range of views and chart patterns of agreement and disagreement in one space. As with any start-up venture, the process wasn't error-free. But in the end, I believe that the conversation met the goal of modeling careful and respectful dialogue across political differences.

Looking back on my participation in the project, I have gained new insights into the nature of political discourse. This short reflection will discuss some of what I have learned from this project, highlighting some of the general barriers to more civil political dialogue, identifying specific strengths and weaknesses of current evangelical policy debates, and offering some suggestions for ways Christians can work individually and together to encourage a more respectful politics.

Some Barriers to Respectful Conversation

Even when people enter a conversation with the best of intentions, the dialogue can break down. Although I was pleased with the quality and tone of most of the postings in the Alternative Political Conversation, I saw some patterns that remind me of the difficulty of the task. What are some of the barriers that impede fruitful discussions of politics?

Complexity

First, and perhaps most important, is the problem of *complexity*. As I like to remind my students, if problems arise that are quick and easy to solve, governments or other organizations quickly step in and do what is needed. The problems that remain in advanced industrialized nations like the United States are the ones that have no readily apparent, simple solutions. To complicate matters further, it is difficult or even impossible to pinpoint the precise causes of many of society's deepest, most persistent problems. It should come as no surprise that we have difficulty engaging in meaningful and civil dialogue about complex problems if the search for solutions is vexing and often incomplete.

My participation in the APC showed me the depth of this problem in new ways. When Harold Heie assigned the first conversation topic, the federal budget deficit, he asked contributors to post 600–800 word essays. Almost immediately we realized that the word length was far too short. Harold adjusted the guidelines to allow 800–1,000 word postings; even so, we continued to face great difficulty scratching the surface of each topic. Many of us exceeded the word limits, and all of us experienced frustration with not having the space to say as much as we would like in such short essays. The interactive nature of the forum helped expand the discussion. Readers often asked clarifying questions and raised significant issues and concerns that the initial responses had ignored due to lack of space. Ultimately, we all found that limits on space and time prevented us from addressing many significant topics and perspectives that would have enriched the discussion.

Talking Past Each Other

Another problem is the tendency to *talk past one another* when discussing politics. Given the complexity of political issues and the wide range of interrelated topics and concepts, it is far too easy to engage in a political conversation without focusing on the same aspects of the larger issue or debate. If conversation partners disagree about a topic but are unable to focus on similar elements at the same time, frustration and chaos soon follow.

Even in the APC, our essays at times seemed to veer in different directions; given a large set of leading questions and such short word limits, some essays focused on one or two aspects of the issue under discussion and ignored others completely. We addressed this problem to some extent with midcourse corrections. For the first set of topics, all contributors posted essays at the same time. For the later topics, half the contributors posted initial essays, and the others posted responses. Even in a focused forum like ours, it was still difficult to engage disagreements directly. In the daily experience of in-person conversations, the complexities only intensify.

Lack of Models

Another common problem worthy of mention is the *lack of models* of respectful political dialogue. Cable news talk shows and the blogosphere are replete with examples of how *not* to engage in political discussion. One need not look far to find shouting matches, anger, disdain, insistent talking past one another, deliberate manipulation of facts, and other displays of disrespect.

Most contemporary political discussions are intended to upset people. Many media personalities, for example, want to make people angry and want to cause alarm as a method of capturing attention and increasing ratings. Those who prefer to model a better way to engage in political conversations find few examples of constructive, positive political dialogue to help them.

Inappropriate Assumptions

A fourth barrier to constructive political discussion is inappropriately *assuming we know another's motives.* In what I believe is one of the big ironies of political discussion, many people automatically assume that those who agree with them have good motives and assume that those who disagree with them have the worst of intentions.

Consider one example: The authors of a recent book on Congress claimed that a Republican member of Congress chose to sleep in his office instead of renting an apartment in DC because he didn't want to be "captured by the evil Capitol culture." In reality, there are several members of Congress who sleep in their offices, but their motives are far from sinister. The one member I know personally who always slept in his office did so because of finances. He had a home back in the district and children in college. He couldn't afford to rent an apartment in Washington. His decision to sleep in his office was a sacrifice he made in the name of public service.

To foster respectful conversation, we should approach political discussions assuming that others are also trying to work toward the common good, that they have good motivations, and that they genuinely want a better world. In other words, we should follow the Golden Rule and treat others as we would want them to treat us. For the most part, the APC postings and responses followed this pattern. We were able to engage one another with respect because we entered the project with a shared commitment to civil and meaningful dialogue.

Evangelicals and Political Discourse: An Appraisal

Writing to the divided church in Corinth, the Apostle Paul exhorts believers to live in a more vibrant and Christ-like community. In 1 Corinthians 13, Paul describes "the most excellent way," which is God's way of love: "Love is patient, love is kind. It does not envy, it does not boast, it is not proud. It does not dishonor others, it is not self-seeking, it is not easily angered, it keeps no record of wrongs. Love does not delight in evil but rejoices with the truth. It always protects, always trusts, always hopes, always perseveres."

How does current evangelical political discourse align with this description of Christian love? Not always so well. In this section, I will identify a few specific problems in contemporary evangelical politics, suggest ideas for improvement, and highlight the work of a few organizations who are modeling a better way.

Areas of Weakness

Far too many religious organizations and spokespeople adopt the same angry tone and disrespectful tactics as their secular counterparts: unkind words, boastful and proud statements, bold attempts to dishonor opponents, and self-promoting tactics. Instead of approaching politics as a form of Christian witness, many evangelicals join in the fray. Indeed, the title of our project, *"Alternative* Political Conversation"* makes this point clear. Civil dialogue, even among Christians, is too often the exception instead of the rule.

Another significant problem in evangelical political discourse is the tendency to belittle opponents within and outside Christianity, both directly and indirectly. When explaining the religious basis for their perspectives, some advocates speak as if their view is *the only* Christian view. Many Christians in politics offer dogmatic pronouncements on complicated and vexing policy matters, acting as if they are God's spokesperson. Such an approach leaves no room for debate or meaningful conversation and implies that all other views are out of line with Christian teaching. In reality, the Bible rarely offers clear direction about what public policy routes are best or worst to pursue; instead, it teaches principles that fallen men and women seek to apply to all of life, including politics. To complicate matters, cultural, personal, and theological assumptions affect the ways in which different believers translate biblical principles into political positions.

Christians should turn to the Bible and church teaching to shape their political perspectives, but they should do so with great humility and awareness of the complexity of the task. Careful study of Scripture reveals God's truth and principles that can guide political debates; the Bible is particularly helpful pointing Christians to end goals that God wants his children to pursue. But much of the content of policy debate centers on *how* to achieve desired goals and *who* (e.g., government, the church, individuals) is best positioned to accomplish them, and the Bible offers much less guidance for how to resolve such debates. In the end, thoughtful and faithful Christians will fundamentally disagree about the best answers to many political questions, so Christian public discourse needs to allow space for this.

Another weakness in many evangelical political discussions is the all-too-common error of conflating ideology and theology. Because the terms "liberal" and "conservative" are commonly used to describe both political ideology and theological commitments, people often confuse the two or assume that they must go together. Political and theological labels can be helpful, but they are often the source of confusion and divisiveness. Christians need to look beyond labels for others and for themselves as a form of Christian witness, for it reflects a commitment to seeing one another as bearers of God's image.

At times Christians use these labels to attack opponents. Stereotypical assumptions about others based on their political ideology—or even just how others label them—fall short of the command to love our neighbors. Instead of quickly dismissing people because they do not appear to share our views, we need to engage them in meaningful conversations that will allow for dialogue and foster mutual respect.

Some Christians believe they should approach their faith as if it were a political ideology. To some extent, this is indeed true and even inescapable, as the Christian faith provides intellectual and ethical guidelines useful for evaluating and interpreting all other ideologies. On the other hand, if Christians apply their faith in such a way that it becomes just another form of political ideology, they risk confusing divine teaching about Christian life and service with specific prescriptions for crafting public policy.

Areas of Strength

Although many barriers and problems complicate the task of respectful political dialogue, evangelicals have a great opportunity to reflect the love of Christ by modeling a different way to listen to and talk with one another about politics. Many followers of Christ heed his important call, acting and speaking in ways that set them apart and point others to Christ.

Religious leaders who make outrageous claims and spew hateful talk draw far too much attention in the news media, but many Christian organizations and individuals are doing important work that brings honor to Christ. Domestically and internationally, faith-based organizations like the Salvation Army, World Vision, World Relief, and Compassion International are making a positive difference meeting human needs. Church-based social service ministries across the United States are caring for people in their communities.

At times, evangelical political discourse seems indistinguishable from secular discourse, but some organizations and individuals are charting a different path. At its best, evangelical political dialogue contributes positively to policy debates, brings new arguments to the discussion, models respect for one another, and points people to Christ. The Center for Public Justice and the Institute for Global Engagement are examples of organizations that model respectful dialogue and encourage thoughtful, faith-informed political debate.

It is all too easy to forget that many faithful Christians serve at all levels of elected office. In my work on Capitol Hill, I was surprised and encouraged to meet so many members of Congress and staff members who were men and women of deep, committed faith. Many elected officials are quietly and faithfully living out the call to love God and neighbor in their daily work. It is encouraging to see people of faith treat their political rivals with dignity and respect, present opposing political positions fairly, address differences with humility and truth, and foster open and constructive dialogue.

Although Christians face great temptations to engage in politics as warfare, some evangelicals have chosen an alternative, and more loving, path. Their work demonstrates that a different kind of politics is possible, one that invites conversation and transformation, not condemnation and suspicion.

Ideas for More Positive Political Dialogue

How can evangelicals and others motivate elected officials to engage in respectful political conversation? Given the state of contemporary political discourse, I am not optimistic that most elected officials and candidates for office will quickly or easily change their ways. The political environment has become so toxic and the distrust between political parties runs so deep that it is hard to see a clear way forward. Some brave men and women adopt a more civil tone and seek genuine partnerships across political divides, but the current incentive structures make such a task very difficult and discouraging.

Likely the best way to encourage more positive political dialogue is to begin with ourselves. Even if we can't transform formal political discourse, we can be significant agents for change in our own lives and in the lives of those closest to us. By modeling respectful dialogue, we show that it is possible to extend grace to others as we talk about politics.

Consider a few examples of practical steps we can take to help navigate political conversations that get heated.

Encourage people to listen to one another and not interrupt. In some political discussions, it seems impossible to finish a sentence, much less explain a complete thought. When talking about different viewpoints, suggest that those with different views take turns explaining what they think. Give each person sufficient time to talk without interruptions, and save questions until after everyone has had an opportunity to express their views.

Seek a neutral moderator. When possible, identify someone among the group who has a gift of resolving conflicts to serve as an informal moderator who can guide the conversation from a more neutral stance.

Respectfully check one another's facts. If someone makes an outrageous or suspicious claim, ask him or her the source of the information. Whenever possible, try to gently but firmly dispel rumors and lies.

Be willing to end a heated conversation. If the conversation gets too heated, it may be best to change the subject. Someone could say, firmly but lovingly, "I can see we have some strong disagreements here, and I don't think we are going to resolve them here. Why don't we talk about another subject for a while. How about those Chicago White Sox?"

Politics is important; political questions address significant issues that directly affect our lives and the lives of millions of others. Many people naturally have strong feelings about politics, and those strong feelings can quickly turn into heated arguments. But it is possible to express our conviction with passion while still showing care and respect.

Concluding Thoughts

God's truth as it unfolds from Genesis to Revelation reveals that all men and women bear God's image, that God loved humanity so much that he gave his Son, and that God's greatest desire is to reconcile people to himself. God wants his children to love and value others, to love their neighbors, and to see his image reflected in his creation. Politics is one arena in which Christians can relate to others in this way, learning from one another's differences and demonstrating respect and love.

We can and should be agents of change, seeking first to transform ourselves and then looking outward to encourage religious leaders and elected officials to adopt a more faithful and respectful politics. The exact ways in which we will seek this transformation will vary, but we can all join together in one essential task: prayer. As Paul reminds us in 1 Timothy 2:1–3: "I urge, then, first of all, that petitions, prayers, intercession and thanksgiving be made for all people—for kings and all those in authority, that we may live peaceful and quiet lives in all godliness and holiness. This is good, and pleases God our Savior."

A central goal of the Alternative Political Conversation was to model a different way of talking about faith and politics. As this book has made clear, in large part the project met its goals, bringing together contributors from a variety of backgrounds and perspectives to share some insights into current political debates. My hope is that this respectful conversation will lead to new opportunities to showcase the diversity of political views within evangelicalism and encourage followers of Christ to approach politics as an essential opportunity for Christian witness.

Speaking the Truth, *in Love*

Paul Brink

In my professional life as a Christian political theorist, both in my teaching and in my research, most of my time is spent in the pursuit of *truth*. Blessed with Christian mentors who have quite deliberately considered how best to undertake this task, I have been encouraged to study the relation between my faith and my academic work. I have pursued with some vigor the question of how certain accepted biblical truths concerning human beings and political life should inform what I learn about politics from my study of creation. With my students, I seek to model how to pursue truth as a Christian scholar—it's important to me that they be able to seek truth in political science in a way that is supported and informed by the biblical narrative of creation, fall, and redemption.

In these respects, I do not believe that I am particularly unusual. Throughout the months of my participation in the Alternative Political Conversation, and as I have read the contributions of my colleagues, I have been able to see and appreciate how their priorities are in many ways similar to my own. While we disagreed on plenty of matters of policy, we could agree on the importance of truth and, very broadly, on how it is to be pursued. Indeed, this I found to be one of the more encouraging aspects of our time together in political conversation, and it provides more evidence to me that the situation of the "evangelical mind" is far less scandalous today than it was when Mark Noll wrote his important book back in 1995.[1]

Knowing Truth, Loving the World

But here is my challenge: While I have personally been encouraged in my Christian academic life concerning the pursuit of truth, and while I believe considerable progress has been made by evangelicals and others in this pursuit over the past several decades, I don't believe that I am very good at actually *talking* about it. I don't have a great many models, and I just don't get much practice. Either I am surrounded by people who basically agree with me on most things, or I am with people who not only disagree with me on the issues at hand, but even disagree as to how we should engage in conversation about them. And when I am in that second situation, all the time and energy that I have spent pursuing truth just does not seem to help me much—indeed, I get the impression that to those around me, I am simply appearing more and more wrong in greater and greater detail.

I suspect that, in this respect also, I am not so unusual. I accepted Harold Heie's invitation to become part of the Alternative Political Conversation project because, like him, I find the state of our political discourse to be deeply discouraging. The vitriolic political conversation, the unwillingness to search for common ground, the lack of sustained conversations about disagreements have resulted in a politics that is dishonoring both to the political actors themselves and to the citizens to whom they are accountable. It also has resulted in a broken

---

[1] Mark Noll, *The Scandal of the Evangelical Mind* (Grand Rapids: Eerdmans, 1995).

political system where vital decisions remain unmade, the possibilities for reform remain elusive, and public justice remains unrealized.

I also accepted Harold's invitation because, regretfully, Christians often are contributing as much to the decline of civility in politics as they are seeking to bring about its healing. Christians think a great deal about truth and a great deal about justice, but they do not often think a great deal about conversation, about how to come alongside people with whom they disagree and engage in respectful dialogue. And when I considered the situation honestly, I had to concede that *I also* think a great deal about truth and a great deal about justice, but not a great deal about conversation, about how to come alongside people with whom I disagree, and seek ways that I might engage in respectful dialogue. This realization I found troubling because it suggests the phenomenon that I decry in politics could be the result of patterns and habits I myself possess.

What are the reasons for these patterns and habits? One possibility may be theological. While the pursuit of truth provides the *subject* of my scholarship, while common grace allows for the *possibility* for interfaith dialogue and scholarship, and while the realities of a democratic politics make it *prudent* to pursue such dialogue, it could be that these together do not provide a sufficient *motive* for Christians to seek the alternative political conversations for which Harold and others are calling.

Why should we engage those with whom we disagree? One reason, perhaps, is to gain access to the truths these others have discovered (the so-called "treasures of the Egyptians" rationale). Or perhaps we engage so that we can join with these others in shaping our social space (especially politically, but also in other ways).

Both of these are true enough, but I wonder if these arguments are insufficient on their own. I find suggestive, in this regard, the idea that we engage in these difficult conversations not primarily to "get something done," either for ourselves or for our society—but simply because these conversation partners are our neighbors. The biblical injunction to love one's neighbor thus applies in our difficult political conversations, as it does everywhere else.

The Christian approach to seeking truth as I have described it places a heavy emphasis on the study of creation in the light of Scripture. This I believe to be an important and valuable distinctive. But taken alone, this can be an approach that overemphasizes a Christian understanding of the world, perhaps at the expense of a Christian way of being in the world. Perhaps we Christians need not only to *understand* the world; we also need to *love* the world. In our studies, in our politics, in our lives, we must seek truth—but we need to seek truth *in love*.[2] This emphasis can perhaps change our perspective of how our conversations with those with whom we have deep disagreements are significant for the kingdom of God.

Disestablishment a Second (or Third? or Fourth?) Time

But the reasons for our difficulties are not only theological; they are also historical and sociological. Although the 500th anniversary of the beginning of the Reformation is only four years away, many Christians still have trouble getting over their establishmentarian habits: we still prefer to speak in the political arena as though the people across the aisle heard the same sermon we did last Sunday.

Meanwhile, others of us are only too aware that Christians are not in the establishment—and so our central preoccupation is to get

---

[2] Ephesians 4:15. Some of the writings of Nicholas Wolterstorff are instructive on these points. See especially his *Educating for Life*, ed. Gloria Goris Stronks and Clarence W. Joldersma (Grand Rapids: Baker, 2002).

back what's ours. And we actually talk that way. One can almost see the alternative political conversation fade away into nothingness.

Perhaps there was a time when it was possible to see U.S. society as "basically Christian." This may have been an ideal realized more in theory than in practice. But it is true that at some time a broadly Christian framework was said to provide, and perhaps actually did provide, the moral backdrop upon which a political conversation could depend. Today, this moral backdrop is no longer present. I suspect one of the reasons U.S. Christianity has, if anything, contributed to the decline in the quality of our political conversation is because it is still coming to terms with the fact that we live in a radically pluralist society.

What has formed the new moral backdrop? The reigning public philosophy in the United States and in most other Western democracies today is political liberalism, an ideological view descended from John Locke that emphasizes the individual and individual rights as the key building block of state and society.

The problem, of course, is that in a society as pluralist as that of the United States, the establishment of political liberalism as the reigning philosophy is as much of a religious establishment as the Christianity it sought to replace. And there can be little doubt that this new establishment has itself undermined the possibility of an alternative political conversation in favor of the liberal conversation that it proposes. In this respect, we can see that Christians are not unique in responding poorly to threats of disestablishment.

Therefore, the theoretical question—one that has great practical implications for the quality of our political conversations—is whether it is possible to imagine a genuinely pluralist politics. Ironically, while Christians and liberals may disagree on a great many things, both groups are likely to agree that successful political conversations require a deep moral consensus that undergirds the state and our political life more generally. Both desire a strong consensus; they merely disagree on its contents. Indeed, it is precisely when political discussions get more challenging that they may seek to tighten the grounds for agreement.

My own view, in contrast, is that we will begin to discover ourselves in genuinely alternative political conversations only when we reject both the Christian and liberal establishments and seek rather a grounding for politics that is as pluralist as the society that surrounds it. In other words, the time is right to pry open the door for approaches to politics less concerned with strong consensus and its achievement and more willing to instead emphasize the importance of plurality in public life, and indeed, to recognize our plurality to be a vital part of our public consciousness.

This approach may require some revision to what we understand to be normal politics. Historically, in the western world, political authority has been justified in terms of a strong societal moral consensus on truth. At a time when that moral consensus fades away, it is tempting for all parties—Christians, liberals, and many others—to attempt to reassert older rules that seemed to offer some security against instability. The breakdown in a strong consensus will appear threatening to those who hold to a "community with shared perspective" vision of politics. Faced by such threats, it's not surprising that possibilities for civil dialogue and respectful conversation fade away.

But the question must be asked: Is it in fact true that what fundamentally holds together a political order is an ideological, religious, or other "strong" agreement among citizens concerning the nature of that order? If this belief is true, then our present situation is truly alarming. However, it is not obviously true. There may be many more things that sustain a political order, most of which have little to do with a strong moral consensus on religious or identity questions.

For example, we might consider a conception of the political that depends upon the willingness of the participants simply to respect, for whatever reason, the basic rules of a constitutional democracy, rather than upon a larger, integrative moral vision for politics that all must share. Of course, we enter into the political fray accompanied by our visions of the true, the just and the beautiful—indeed, politics can be about contests of visions of politics, as about anything else. But the basic constitutional guarantee of democratic participation is more important than a prior agreement concerning the moral grounds for that participation.

Can alternative political conversations be possible in such an environment? I think so—and in ways that are healthier and more open than we encounter currently. Ultimately, the answer to that question may depend on our willingness to let go of the terms of the conversation and to give up the concern that our conversation proceed on "our" common basis.

Once we have done so, the possibility for respectful conversation draws closer, as people can come to agreement on particular points or conclusions or policies without agreeing on the underlying reasons for those points or conclusions or policies. Indeed, we might even see this plurality as a strength, rather than a weakness, recognizing the plural bases of support as a sign of widespread endorsement for the political enterprise.

The Ethics of Alternative Political Conversations

From a Christian perspective, one clear advantage of this approach to alternative political conversations is that it allows for a genuinely Christian voice. Christians can speak from their position of truth without being required to translate their arguments into a language not their own in order to be heard. Christians can take part in the conversation as Christians. But just as significantly, neither are Christians requiring others to abandon their own voices as a condition for speaking. And from the perspective I described above, of seeking truth and loving the world, these are very great goods indeed.

I believe this approach may allow new possibilities in our dialogue, a widening of our conversations beyond their current limits. For example, progress on many of our political debates remains elusive because of our preoccupation with (and misunderstanding of) individual rights. The classical liberal view that the very purpose of government is the preservation of rights very easily turns any political conversation into the mere assertion of claims for competing rights.

The consequences are troubling. The high view of human dignity found in the Christian tradition, for instance, loses a great deal of its moral force when translated into liberal rights-talk. It also loses a great deal of its potential as a contributor to our political discussion. The Christian tradition has been one that has emphasized respect for human dignity, also in the form of rights, but has insisted that rights be paired with responsibilities and individual freedoms paired with the obligation to ensure respect for the full freedoms of other individuals and organizations.

If we believe, for example, that human dignity requires the right to bear arms, that same foundation of human dignity requires regulations to ensure this right is appropriately related to all the other rights and responsibilities we bear. Finding ways to incorporate this and other fuller accounts of human rights and responsibilities is one positive outcome of opening up our political discourse.

Of course I do not mean to imply that such conversations will be easy. Indeed, they may often be difficult as we are encouraging our conversation partners to participate with all their convictional particularities intact. One of the results of my participation in the Alternative Political Conversation project has been that I have begun considering what might be called the "ethics of alternative political conversations." What qualities should characterize our participation in these conversations? What might we consider to be pluralist political virtues? What are our responsibilities in this conversation, both as people who listen and people who speak?

For instance, when we *listen* to others in our political conversation, we cannot insist upon certain modes of argument or certain conceptions of reason as conditions for speaking with us—that is, we cannot require other participants to borrow a language not their own in order to speak to us. But does this go further? In a pluralist society, can we discount the *political* merits of a particular position merely because it is premised upon different grounds than our own? It seems to me that we should not do so; rather, we must consider whether or how that particular position might be supported by grounds that we ourselves hold, even in ways that perhaps none of us expected.

Similarly, when we *speak*, we might consider whether there exists an obligation that we make clear our motivating or justifying reasons when we make a political argument, or whether it might be appropriate instead to choose to keep silent about those motivating reasons. We also might consider the reverse situation: If one makes an argument using language entirely from within a particular religious view, is there some sort of obligation to make clear the *political* implications of that religious view? This would seem to make strategic sense if we're trying to persuade others, but is there some sort of requirement that we do so?

The Illustration of Abortion Discussions

Consider the difficult case of abortion as an illustration of this second set of concerns. Abortion provides an example of an issue where civility is frequently the exception rather than the rule. What we hear are strong, defiant statements of principle, expressed in "here, I take my stand" tones, and full-throated rejections of alternative points of view. Civility is frequently an early casualty in this form of political discourse.

But as we consider the ethics of an alternative political conversation, we might note that in a properly civil discussion, statements of political principle normally require justification. My sense is that in a society where there is so much disagreement about moral foundations, and in a model of political discourse that discourages introducing these controversial moral foundations, we are often encouraged, explicitly or implicitly, to *avoid* explaining why we hold the moral positions we do. We simply expect others to disagree with those foundations or even assume that others simply cannot understand these motivating reasons.

And so we have pro-life supporters arguing their position as though it descended upon them from the sky, and we see pro-choice advocates repeating the "right to abortion" mantra as though a rights claim isn't also a moral claim that needs to be considered alongside other moral claims. Essentially, we believe we must censor ourselves. The result is the loss of a genuinely principled public discussion, and ultimately a loss for all sides.

In the abortion debate, we can also encounter the reverse situation. Pro-life advocates occasionally are very clear on how their position on abortion is informed by their religious commitments but not at all clear on what they believe to be the political implications of that commitment. Psalm 139, for example, may reveal that "you knit me together in my mother's womb," but this is still a good distance from a political argument that might be offered by a Christian legislator. Making clear the political implications of our religious views is important if we are hoping to make progress in our conversations.

Is Agreement Possible?

Can we actually come to agreements in such conversation situations? Again, much depends on the willingness of the participants to let go of the terms of the debate and give up their concern to proceed on a common moral basis. In pluralist societies, we must tolerate, even celebrate, agreements that do not go "all the way down."

From the Christian perspective, I believe this to be model of conversation that can be embraced. If we can understand *justice* to require that all members of society have the ability to participate in our common life, then it seems that the Christian conception of *society* is of an "open society," in which men and women have the right to reach out to God or to what they consider to be their final transcendent value. In other words, the state does not merely tolerate faith; it does not grant "exemptions" or even "rights" to faith. Rather, it acknowledges what faith is and creates space for its expression. This understanding of faith and politics gives us some clues for considering the nature of our obligations to others in the public space—and especially our obligations to those with whom we have deep disagreements.

A favorite theorist of mine, Bernard Crick, has said of politics that it "is not, then, a grasping for the ideal; but neither is it the freezing of tradition. It is an activity—lively, adaptive, flexible, and conciliatory."[3] This definition comes close to describing what this alternative

---

[3] Bernard Crick, *In Defence of Politics*, 2nd ed. (Harmondsworth, U.K.: Penguin, 1986), 56.

political conversation might be like. And it reminds us that, in the Christian perspective, we ought not to expect an ultimate political consensus ever and that if we are to look for a final point of reference and source of authority, it can only be found *beyond* society.[4] All politics is kingdom politics, but politics is not itself ultimate—we need to talk about it that way.

---

[4] Bernard Zylstra, "The Bible, Justice and the State," *International Reformed Bulletin* 5 (1973): 13.

A New Era in Evangelical Public Engagement?

DAVID P. GUSHEE

It has been my pleasure to be involved in this Alternative Political Conversation, so nicely shepherded by Harold Heie, for whom I have the deepest respect and gratitude.

I believe the results you have seen in the foregoing pages reveal what is possible when thoughtful people engage in "respectful conversation" along the lines attempted in this effort. The results so far transcend our smash-mouth politics in Congress, talk radio, and niche politico-entertainment TV that it is hard to believe we are all engaged in the same enterprise.

Perhaps, in a sense, we are not. One striking characteristic of evangelical Christianity, across our own ideological spectrum, is a kind of *wholesome earnestness*. Whether visiting Liberty University or Wheaton College, Baker Books or World Vision, the Christian Community Development Association or the National Association of Evangelicals, the Ukrainian Evangelical Theological Seminary in Kiev or the Evangelical Theological Faculty of Croatia, an observer cannot help but notice this characteristic quality of wholesome earnestness. As a somewhat late arriver to evangelical Christianity, it was one of the first things that I noticed.

You see, evangelicals still believe in God. And we believe in Jesus Christ. And we believe in what someone has called a "purpose-driven life." We believe that we are supposed to be about important things in the world that go beyond our self-interest. We believe that God is also about important things in the world, a project that Jesus taught us to call the kingdom of God.

This wholesome earnestness makes us strangers to those for whom politics is merely a winner-take-all game, or those who get their jollies out of verbal cruelty on air or in print, or those who merely use politics to advance corporate self-interest, or those who just simply crave power, or those who just want to get reelected.

The emergence of U.S. evangelicals from political quietism in the 1960s into forceful public engagement brought an enormous amount of moral energy (a.k.a., wholesome earnestness) into public life in the country. And this occurred precisely at the time that the United States as a whole was becoming more secular, cynical, and committed to selfish projects of authenticity and self-actualization.

But as most everyone who follows U.S. politics or evangelical religion now knows, evangelicals ended up fragmenting politically. As David Swartz has now clearly shown in his important book, *Moral Minority*,[1] the evangelical "first responders" into the chaotic political scene of the late 1960s and 1970s were evangelical progressives such as Mark Hatfield, Jim Wallis, and Ron Sider. Only later did Jerry Falwell, Pat Robertson, Ralph Reed, James Dobson, and others create a Christian Right and marry it so tightly to the Republican Party. From the era of Ronald Reagan to the second term of George W. Bush, this Christian Right gobbled up headlines and came to dominate

---

[1] David Swartz, *The Evangelical Left in an Age of Conservatism: Politics and Culture in Modern America* (Philadelphia: University of Pennsylvania Press, 2012).

public perceptions of evangelical political engagement. Meanwhile, the activists of the Left continued plugging away, nurturing their smaller, less visible organizations in relative obscurity until, I would argue, the decline of Bush and the rise of Barack Obama. At that time, a concerted effort on the part of the Democratic Party to be, or appear to be, more faith-friendly, together with the skillful writing and organizing of Jim Wallis, served to bring these groups back into view.

In my own professional journey since 1990, I have been deeply immersed in the evangelical Left (perhaps Center-Left), and have been a robust critic of the Christian Right. I have believed that the Left better reflected the moral commitments of the Jesus of the New Testament and of the Hebrew prophets whose ministry he so clearly culminated.

But even while writing my 2008 book, *The Future of Faith in American Politics,*[2] in which my political engagement at that level crested, it became clear to me that most of the enormous quantity of writing and advocacy and media work done by the most visible voices on the right and the left lacked the intellectual depth that can emerge only from trained political scientists, policy analysts, and social ethicists. There are fine, fine nuggets of moral reflection and policy advocacy in those artifacts of the evangelical culture wars; meanwhile, and often under their inspiration, a whole generation of evangelicals had gone to school to tackle policy issues at a far deeper level with the tools available in contemporary academia.

These are the kinds of voices represented in this collection (my training in such matters is more humble than my colleagues here, I

---

[2] David Gushee, *The Future of Faith in American Politics: The Public Witness of the Evangelical Center* (Waco, Texas: Baylor University Press, 2008).

assure you). They represent the maturing of evangelical political science and policy analysis over the last generation. Many of them—and the spirit of the overall collection—draw on the conceptual frameworks developed in neo-Calvinist/Kuyperian political ethics, one of the most robust, distinctively evangelical intellectual traditions that exists today. And notice the schools they represent: Wheaton, Gordon, Calvin, Pepperdine, Azusa Pacific, etc. These are bread-and-butter evangelical universities.

So my answer to the question of how to assess the current state of evangelical public policy discourse is this: if one looks to the intellectually robust, secularly trained yet Christianly-shaped authors who contributed to this collection, and one considers that these are the women and men who are teaching the political science classes in some of our best Christian colleges and universities, there is considerable reason for optimism. Meanwhile, generational transition in the most visible Christian advocacy organizations, together with stark political changes in U.S. culture, may mean that fresh winds will also emerge from long-time veterans of public engagement and their organizations.

Perhaps such changes in the evangelical community can play a role in motivating our elected political representatives to move toward more respectful political discourse and thus, perhaps, better policymaking. To the extent that evangelicals have been known for strident, polemical, and disrespectful politicking coupled with shallow policy thinking, we have contributed to the problem. But it is hard for me to believe that the evangelicals trained at Council for Christian Colleges and Universities (CCCU) campuses, such as those mentioned, will favor firebrands in politics, if they have any say in the matter.

Already, thoughtful college graduates from such institutions are beginning to try their hand at advocacy and electoral politics. Perhaps part of the coming of age of contemporary evangelicals under the age of thirty-five will be attempting to make an impact in marginalizing the flamethrowers as well as advocating for reforms in our electoral system—for example, nonpartisan redistricting—that will reward those who are willing to govern from the middle rather than the left or right edges. Their well-informed "wholesome earnestness" could make a profound difference in our politics. Let us hope so.

Reviewing Harold Heie's synthesis of the stimulating issue conversations we participated in over nine months, I was impressed by what we collectively achieved in terms of respectful conversation and in terms of finding areas of common ground. I only regret that international travel obligations kept me out of the conversations on several issues.

Looking back now from a distance at the 2012 presidential election, certain issues have become clearer, and some have taken on a new look. The enforced budget sequester is actually imposing a measure of meat-cleaver discipline on the budget, and a tax increase was also pushed through by President Obama just after the election. Quite despite itself, Washington seems to be uncooperatively managing a few steps in the right direction. However, the grand bargain that would deal with entitlement programs seems beyond our reach, and we still lurch from crisis to crisis.

Immigration reform appears almost inevitable as I write, in part because the rising power of the Latino/Latina vote, together with the Republican shellacking in that demographic, is enforcing some kind of near consensus in Washington. Thus it may be proven that miracles still do happen.

The Health and Human Services contraception mandate may well head to the Supreme Court, despite further administrative tinkering with the rules that has occurred since these essays were written. The Court has the opportunity to offer significant doctrinal clarification on church/state issues with its ruling. I am not sure what I now believe about the adequacy of the current proposed regulations.

Talk of war with Iran has faded, while the desperate unraveling of Syria has now cost 70,000 lives. The United States is edging away from non-involvement in Syria's civil war, but there is little stomach here for a direct military intervention. Peace between Israel and a future Palestine seems farther away than ever, in my view, mainly because Israeli hardliners are gradually achieving a creeping annexation of the West Bank and East Jerusalem. The situation seems even more intractable than is revealed in these pages.

The U.S. economy is improving, and some college graduates are actually finding jobs. But corporations are sitting on huge piles of money as the stock market goes through the roof. Meanwhile, a disastrous one-fifth of the country's population is permanently left behind, living in neighborhoods and going to schools that no reader of this collection would tolerate for a minute.

Gay marriage is advancing in public opinion and ballot initiatives. The Republican Party is divided between those trying to hold the line and those ready to throw in the towel. The Supreme Court will decide two cases in 2013 that may resolve the issue once and for all—or may not. I personally believe it's time for evangelicals to support a pragmatic policy solution that recognizes and therefore stabilizes same-sex relationships, especially for the sake of the many thousands of children already embedded in such families. And yes, they are families. I know several of them. And they do not appear interested in settling for the half-measure of civil unions.

Health-care reform is being implemented, and many Republican governors have decided to play ball with the administration, accepting insurance exchanges and Medicaid money. There is some evidence that the health-care cost curve is beginning to bend a bit. Hopefully, innovative experiments fostered by the Affordable Care Act, together with intense political pressure, will keep attention focused on ways to create more affordable health care for all.

After Newtown, the demand for a wide array of policy and cultural responses related to gun violence became a crescendo. Bills are making their way through Congress. But as I write some of these are already being weakened. Perhaps we will get enhanced background checks. The power of the NRA—and its friends in government—to kill commonsense gun legislation remains terribly evident.

The reelection of Barack Obama means that current abortion law, based on *Roe v. Wade* as slightly modified by *Planned Parenthood v. Casey*, will remain the law of the land for the foreseeable future. Meanwhile, out of frustration, states are passing largely symbolic anti-abortion legislation that will never survive court challenges. And no one is talking much about consensus abortion-reduction measures.

Theoretical discussions about the proper size and role of government may be getting a boost because of worries over the use of remotely-piloted drones to kill people (including Americans) abroad and possibly to monitor us here at home quite soon. Kentucky senator Rand Paul, a Republican, created quite a stir with a filibuster related to drones. Meanwhile, it was quite clear during the 2012 presidential campaign that weariness with our government's constant resort to war was widespread, especially among its young, damaged veterans and their families. More broadly, the defeat of the Romney-Ryan ticket, and the retention of the Senate by the Democrats, means there will be no serious reconsideration of the responsibilities and role of the U.S. government over against civil society and other entities—at least, none that is not driven by budget constraints.

And so the beat goes on. Wholesome, earnest evangelicals continue to reflect on these matters and make our best contributions. We yearn for dramatic progress and hope for modest change. And we await the perfection of this world that will occur when Christ returns.

Continuing the Political Conversation

LISA SHARON HARPER

In his introductory chapter, Harold Heie is careful to point out that the views expressed in this book do not reflect the beliefs of all evangelical Christians, adding that "if another group of evangelical Christians had undertaken this conversation project, the views expressed could have been significantly different." He also hopes that the content of this book will be a "starting point for continuing the conversation."

Heie's hope raises the question of who should be encouraged to continue this political conversation. The six contributors to this APC were chosen to represent various self-designated positions across the political spectrum because the project's main goals were to model respectful conversation among those on different sides of the political aisle and to demonstrate that such respectful conversation can uncover common ground and illuminate remaining differences that beg for ongoing conversation (with the grandiose hope that our political representatives will sit up and take notice and do likewise).

But there are more aspects of our social locations other than how we situate ourselves along the political spectrum. For example, those encouraged to continue the conversation can reflect a diversity of races and ethnicities, or of economic status, or world-view commitments (religious or secular). As Heie points out, there is no way of telling what the results of such continuing conversations may be. But in this postscript, I would like to reflect on what might emerge if the new conversation partners included a healthy balance of white and black evangelicals.

Contrasting Emphases in the White and Black Evangelical Communities

Evangelicals in the United States are at a turning point. We are experiencing a level of cooperation and collaboration across the spectrum of evangelicalism on common-ground issues in a way we have not experienced for nearly a century. Issues like immigration reform, modern-day slavery, and poverty are driving evangelicals to Scripture, and Scripture is compelling us to take action.

Coalitions like the Evangelical Immigration Table have brought together evangelical organizations such as Sojourners, the National Association of Evangelicals (NAE) and the Southern Baptist Convention that rarely (if ever) found themselves in the same room together only a few years ago. As a result, relationships are being forged, and those organizations are finding that their members and leaders share common ground: They follow the same Jesus. They care about immigrants. And they agree there is a proper role for government in the work of doing good.

These new alliances have forged new relationships that have compelled them to press for just policy together in other arenas, as well. For example, the common ground of love for the poor in public policy-making brought together the network called The Circle of Protection, an ecumenical alliance of national Christian organizations that includes both the NAE and Sojourners, among other organizations like the U.S. Conference of Catholic Bishops, Bread for the World, the Evangelical Lutheran Church in America (ELCA), and the Salvation Army. This partnership has made a profound impact on national budgetary policy since 2011 when it began to press Congress and the U.S. church to place a "circle of protection" around the poor in the midst of ideologically driven federal budget wars.

But evangelicals still have a long way to go. On April 15, 2013, during the Christian Churches Together (CCT) in the USA launch of its "Response to Dr. Martin Luther King's Letter from Birmingham Jail," Dr. Ron Sider (founding president of Evangelicals for Social Action) spoke about the culpability of evangelicals in the sin of racism in the United States: "Evangelicals still see racism," he said, "through the lens of the personal and fail to understand the impact of systems and structures on whole people groups."

Evangelical sociologists Christian Smith and Michael Emerson provide evidence for Sider's assertion in their book, *Divided by Faith: Evangelical Religion and the Problem of Race in America.*[1] Employing the sociological theory of cultural toolkits, developed by Ann Swidler, Emerson and Smith found that many evangelicals have three and only three cultural tools that they use to understand the world; rugged individualism, relationalism, and antistructuralism. Many black and white evangelicals share two of the three same tools: individualism and relationalism.

Evangelicals tend to believe salvation is granted to individuals, not communities. Salvation is granted to those who exercise individual agency and choose to accept Jesus' death on the cross as payment for their individual sins. One finding of Emerson and Smith's study,

---

[1] Christian Smith and Michael Emerson, *Divided by Faith: Evangelical Religion and the Problem of Race in America* (New York, Oxford University Press, 2000).

which analyzed data collected from 2,000 phone interviews and 300 face-to-face visits, was that many black evangelicals also employed the tool of rugged individualism. Stress tends to be placed on the individual's ability to overcome sin, brokenness, and struggle. As a result, like their white counterparts, black evangelicals' conception of faith is a primary shaper of a world view that interprets the world through the lens of individualism.

Likewise, evangelical faith centers the locus of the meaning of salvation, not on a set of principles, but on a central relationship, the relationship between God and the individual. It is not enough for an evangelical to believe a set of principles to be saved. One does not get saved from believing wrong things. One is saved from a state of separation from God through the act of believing.

This central tenant of Christian faith, according to Emerson and Smith, has profoundly shaped the world views of many evangelicals. Employing the cultural tool of "relationalism," many black and white evangelicals interpreted the world through the lens of relationships, Emerson and Smith found.

In my book, *Evangelical Does Not Equal Republican . . . or Democrat*,[2] which explored evangelical cultural tools and their impact on evangelical politics, I found no greater example of the "relational" tool at work than in the Promise Keepers movement. In the mid-1990s Promise Keepers set out to solve the problem of racism in America. Its lone strategy was to build relationships between white and black men and other men of color. This strategy ultimately failed because of the third and last tool that Emerson and Smith discovered in white evangelicals cultural toolkit: antistructuralism. Here

---

[2] Lisa Sharon Harper, *Evangelical Does Not Equal Republican ... or Democrat* (New York: The New Press, 2008).

is where black and white evangelicals tended to diverge. Emerson and Smith explain that while many white evangelicals consistently employed the cultural tool of antistructuralism, most black evangelicals did not. A strong tendency among black evangelicals, which is often missing among white evangelicals, is to embrace the tool of "structuralism" that emphasizes "the impact of systems and structures on whole people groups" (to quote Ron Sider once again). And there is a good reason for this contrast. Unlike the experience of most white evangelicals, many black evangelicals have experienced the destructive effect of evil systems and structures on their well-being over numerous years.

This difference is borne out in the Emerson and Smith study. White evangelicals typically demonstrated active hostility toward the notion that systems and structures could hold any bearing on the course of the experiences of an individual, a family, or a people group in the world. The study concluded that the core reason for this vehement push-back is that white evangelicals tend to live above the negative impact of structures and systems.

In the United States of America, a nation with deep Puritan roots and a web of laws and social structures crafted throughout its early history with remnants and repercussions reverberating to the present, most structures and systems were built to support and protect the lives and livelihoods of white people. Thus, as a people group, white Americans in the United States have not had to bear the brunt of unjust systems crafted to keep the group down. In general, they have not been forced to bow as a group under the pressure of oppressive law. Black people—evangelical or not—have.

So herein lies the difference. While white evangelicals in the Emerson and Smith study demonstrated violent opposition to the notion that structures can make even the slightest impact on people groups, black evangelicals tended to understand the impact of systems and structures on people groups. To grasp the power of systems to oppress black evangelicals, you need only to remember the legacy of the intricate webs of law and economic and social structures mounted under the two-hundred-year reign of slavocracy in the antebellum South or the nearly hundred-year reign of Jim Crow after ten glorious years of Reconstruction following the Civil War.

Why have I diverged into a discussion of sociology in a book about politics? Because world view is shaped by both our faith and our experience of the world and world view impacts politics. In my book, *Evangelical Does Not Equal Republican...or Democrat*, I submit the theory that white evangelical use of the tool of antistructuralism can account for the vast gulf between black and white evangelical voters. I found that both groups care about political issues that focus on individual agency and its impact on relationships (think abortion and same-sex marriage). But, while many white evangelicals have limited their circle of public concern to these two issues in the latter third of the twentieth century, black evangelicals have held these issues of public concern along with calls for federal, state, and municipal intervention to address domestic poverty, environmental injustice, health disparity, educational disparity, the impact of the nation's prison industrial complex on black families, the disparate impact of war on black communities, and the web of late twentieth-century drug laws that have crushed generations of black boys and broken black families in the post-civil rights era.

White and Black Evangelicals in Conversation

According to Emerson and Smith's study, the only way they found that white evangelicals suffering from antistructuralism lost that tool was to be immersed in the black community, or other communities of color, for a significant period of time. Those whites who had experienced such immersion answered questions in a vastly different way than did their counterparts. They recognized the impact of laws, systems, and structures on people groups and answered survey questions much like black evangelicals.

Fortunately, as we move through the first decades of the twenty-first century, we see some early signs of such immersion. The suburbs are becoming more diverse. According to a 2011 study by the Brookings Institute, "Melting Pot Cities and Suburbs: Racial and Ethnic Change in Metro America in the 2000s,"[3] as of 2010, 51 percent of all blacks in the United States lived in the suburbs. The same study explains that while whites made up 81 percent of suburban residents in 1990, they now make up only 65 percent. Whether in the city or in the suburbs, white evangelicals are having more and more contact with people who are ethnically unlike them and who have different relationships with the systems that govern society. This heightened level of integration, along with the evangelical movement among evangelical college students to immerse themselves in urban centers for weeks and years, is shaving away at the tool of antistructuralism within evangelical America. And that is cause for hope.

The content of this book confirms that good news is emerging in the twenty-first century. The other contributors to this book, all of them white evangelicals, do not limit their public policy concerns to abortion and same-sex marriage. And in their analyses of many of the public policy issues that we addressed (most notably poverty in the United States, K–12 education, gun control, and the role of government), they address the deleterious effect of broken societal

---

[3] William H. Frey, "Melting Pot Cities and Suburbs: Racial and Ethnic Change in Metro America in the 2000s," www.brookings.edu/media/research/files/papers/2011/05/04-census-ethnicity-frey, May 4, 2011.

systems and structures. But I cannot help but wonder if some of my fellow contributors would have addressed these negative effects and offered more significant positive legal, systemic and structural solutions if they had walked for an extended season in the shoes of black evangelicals. My wondering about this possibility leads to my proposal for continuing the political conversation that the APC project started.

A viable direction that I would like to propose is for the conversation reported on in this book to be continued with the creation of more forums for conversation that include a healthy balance of white and black evangelicals. Such ongoing conversations may significantly heighten and add to the concerns about addressing broken societal systems and structures that are addressed in this book. But, as Harold Heie likes to say, "you can't predict beforehand the results of a genuine conversation."

Of course, that is only one strategy for continuing the political conversation that has been started by this project. I hope, along with Harold Heie, that ongoing forums for respectful political conversation will be created that involve conversation partners representing other races and ethnicities, as well as people who differ in economic status and who hold to differing world-view commitments (religious or secular).

Religious Beliefs in Public Conversations

Stephen V. Monsma

I was puzzling over what to write for this postscript when *New York Times* columnist Frank Bruni came to my rescue. In a column on religion and the difficult issues surrounding same-sex marriage, he wrote that the idea God does not favor same-sex marriage "is probably the most stubborn barrier to the full acceptance of gay and lesbian Americans, a last bastion and engine of bigotry."[1] So much for civil discourse and respectful conversations. "If you have disagreements with me, and especially if they are rooted in traditional religious beliefs, you are a bigot" is hardly the way to engage in respectful conversation.

Even though the essays in this volume do in fact model Christians engaging in respectful conversations from different points on the political spectrum, much of the world—including some *New York Times* columnists—still do not get it. In a broken world, marred by sin, that is not surprising. A certainty in one's own opinions, an arrogant unwillingness to listen to and perhaps learn from others, a commitment to advancing one's esteem in the eyes of others, and

---

[1] Frank Bruni, "Reading God's Mind," *New York Times* (March 5, 2013), A23.

a desire for career advancement all too often trump a desire to find common ground and understand why others have a different point of view.

This seems to be particularly true when religious beliefs and perspectives are introduced into public discussions—the very intent of this "respectful conversation" project. A basic reason for this was revealed in comments made by the MSNBC commentator Steve Kornacki, in a laudatory essay he wrote following the death of C. Everett Koop, an evangelical Christian and the surgeon general under President Ronald Reagan.[2] Kornacki praised Koop for his fights against smoking and HIV-AIDS. At the end of his essay, he offered this strange but revealing sentence: "But his [Koop's] personal moral views never clouded his judgment or his commitment to public health."

I call this sentence strange because anyone who knew Koop or had read his writings would know that his battles against smoking and HIV-AIDS, as well as those against abortion and for better medical care for newborn infants all sprang directly from his "personal moral views." It was his faith in a God who created human beings as his image bearers, and thereby endowed them with incalculable worth, that drove Koop in his various efforts to protect human life and combat that which would shorten it. Koop's Christian, moral views shaped his judgments (or "clouded" his judgments, to use Kornacki's pejorative word).

I call this sentence revealing because it helps explain why many find it difficult to maintain a civil dialogue when we Christians refer

---

[2] Steve Kornacki, "Remembering C. Everett Koop, a Man of Faith – and Science," MSNBC. com, accessed March 5, 2013, www.msnbc.com/2013/02/27/remembering-c-everett-koop-man-of-faith-and-science. Michael Gerson, in a March 5, 2013, *Washington Post* column drew attention to this essay by Steve Kornacki.

to our faith as helping to shape or form our views on public policy issues. They are written off as illegitimate attempts to introduce something that is irrational and has no place in public discourse. Confine your religious views to your churches and your homes! In the public life of the nation, they are no more than exercises in bigotry.

Given these attitudes, is this book and the essays we exchanged during the 2012 election season exercises in futility? I think not. Together they clearly make two important points: (1) religiously-based beliefs and perspectives can shape and inform positions on public policy issues in a thoughtful, rational manner; and (2) Christians who disagree on exactly how religiously-based beliefs and perspectives should shape and inform public policy positions can do so in a civil, respectful manner. And these accomplishments are nothing to disparage. Models, or examples, can be powerful teachers. One could rail against the Brunis and the Kornackis of the world in abstract terms; however, examples of actually doing in a thoughtful, civil manner what they fail to do are likely to have a much greater effect.

But how do we make this point to the wider world of political commentators and elected officials? How can we nudge them in the direction of more respectful discourse and more acceptance of the legitimacy of Christian-based perspectives on public policy issues? There is, of course, no magic answer that will accomplish this in one swipe.

But, ever the optimist, I believe there is hope. At the heart of the Christian faith is the message that Christ has come and that his work of redeeming a fallen world is ongoing. My hope and my prayer is that this book and the essays, perspectives, and applications it contains may serve as a model that will send out ripples, first to the church and then from a renewed church into the broader world. That may sound overly optimistic, even foolishly and naively so, but as I wrote, earlier examples can be powerful teachers. It is up to our God to determine what impact these essays will have. But he is at work in our world, and he is infinitely powerful.

An Example for
the Next Generation

Eric Teetsel

When I was first approached about participating in the Alternative Political Conversation, I was hesitant to say yes. The list of contributors included some of the most influential voices in evangelical academic circles, women and men with advanced degrees in political science and other related fields. Further adding to my trepidation was the size of the task presented: regular essays on virtually every contemporary political issue, from fiscal philosophy to foreign affairs and social policy.

As the voice of the "Far Right" in the conversation and the only contributor under thirty, I challenged myself to take advantage of the opportunity to speak on behalf of a demographic to which I belong and to which I have devoted my professional career. So, outgunned and ill-prepared, I jumped on board.

I graduated from Wheaton College in 2006 and immediately began a master's program at Azusa Pacific University. Soon I took a job at Colorado Christian University, and then the American Enterprise Institute (AEI), and recently at the Manhattan Declaration. Each of these experiences has helped me understand the current state of evangelical political discourse, but especially the way young evangelicals, commonly called Millennials, think about the relationship between faith and culture.

One story from my tenure with the values and capitalism project at AEI illustrates well what's going on. I was explaining to an intern the tension that exists between modernity and Christianity and the implications of that discord for our work. Nodding along, she interrupted my eloquent lecture: "Yeah, it's like, we go to church, but we also watch *The Daily Show*."

Exactly.

The troublesome relationship between Christianity and its cultural surroundings is nothing new. A chunk of the New Testament is devoted to instructions for churches in Galatia, Ephesus, Philippi, and Rome struggling to figure out what it means, exactly, to be "Christian." Some two thousand years later, the church continues to struggle with similar questions. But there's a twist. The sect went viral. Some folks got on a boat and established a new nation based on the idea that human beings were endowed by God with inalienable rights. The script was flipped: Christianity was no longer about carving out a unique witness in the midst of pagan culture but about preserving the Christian story in a somewhat theistic one.

Or, as that intern might put it, there's a showdown: orthodoxy versus Oprah-doxy.

There was a time when ideas were taken seriously, considered carefully, and implemented cautiously. When Abraham Lincoln ran against Stephen Douglas, they engaged in debate seven times in three months. Each time, one candidate would speak for sixty minutes, the other would give a ninety-minute response, followed by a thirty-minute rejoinder. The nation was captivated.

More recently, William F. Buckley's *Firing Line* gave the stalwart grandfather of the modern conservative movement opportunity to engage in lengthy dialogue and debate with leading intellectuals in a variety of fields ranging from politics to literature. In 1988, the show was reduced from sixty minutes to thirty; in 2000, Buckley stepped down.

Intellectual curiosity still exists in pockets in the United States, but more common is a pseudointellectual curiosity of the sort evidenced by Sunday-morning talk shows, Sudoku, and Starbucks. One need not explore the history and heritage of furniture to give the appearance of taste; just go to Pottery Barn.

More common still is intellectual abandonment. Americans, especially the Millennials, feel first and think second. They stumble through life gut first. Such e-motion stems from a culture that preaches, "Baby, you were born that way," subsidized by mediating social institutions—families, schools, churches—built on shifting sand. The result is an ever-expanding nanny state that refuses to allow its chicks to experience and learn from negative consequences.

Orthodoxy requires the cultivation of what my professors at Wheaton used to call "the life of the mind." When considering an issue, orthodoxy lays out our first principles and nonnegotiable truths, creating a framework through which the merits of ideas can be considered and their consequences evaluated.

Oprah-doxy allows us to respond to issues without the hard work of cold, time-consuming consideration. Instead, we start with a base set of emotions, positive and negative. Love, justice, inclusion, authenticity, and equality are good; judgment, intellectual rigidity, and stratification are bad. Feelings toward people and ideas are determined accordingly.

Millennial evangelicals—those who go to church and watch *The Daily Show*—want desperately to interface seamlessly in U.S. culture. But they also want to contribute to society in a positive way, one of the many positive traits of their generation. Unfortunately, the confluence of these traits has led to some questionable outcomes.

It used to be that one could simply care for someone or something. Not anymore. Today, your evangelicals have a *passion* for coffee-plantation workers in Peru. Is that just a fad, driven by social cues and peer influence unrelated to one's Christian faith?

Indeed, among evangelical Millennials, passion—and the actions that flow from such passion—looks and sounds a lot like fashion. This is life according to Oprah-doxy, not the precepts of Scripture.

The Alternative Political Conversation points the way toward a richer, deeper, and more Christian form of cultural engagement, one that gets down to the root issue of the reasons underlying a given passion. There are good reasons to care for coffee workers.

The "why" behind our work matters as much as the work itself. The "why" influences our approach to the work, our goals, and the metrics by which we determine success. Indulging our cravings for consumption and cultural cachet on the premise of Christian love seems to me a dangerous game. Such an approach need not be considered with outcomes for the recipients of so-called good deeds. More fundamentally, it's not an act born of love.

Alternatively, exploring the business of global coffee manufacturing and trade, identifying areas of unfairness or inefficiency, and fixing them so as to provide net benefits to impoverished growers is an expression of Christian love. We love our neighbor by seeking her/his best, and we love God by applying our hearts and minds to the task before us.

Though I think the tendency toward Oprah-doxy is a net benefit for the political Left, APC shows Christians can think and arrive at conclusions that span the spectrum of contemporary American politics. This is our responsibility, as believers called to love God with our whole selves, including our brains.

Though I continue to hold very different opinions from my friends, I learned from them and continue to wrestle with many of their insights, arguments, and questions. My hope is that APC will continue for many years to come as we engage one another through writing and panel discussions. May these experiences serve as examples to the next generation that no matter the opinion you hold, achieve it—don't merely land on it.

Appendix

CONVERSATION GUIDELINES

"It is by no means easy to hold beliefs for which you would be willing to die, and yet to remain open to new insights; but it is precisely such a combination of commitment and inquiry that constitutes religious maturity." —**Ian Barbour**

Guidelines for Respectful Conversation

Provide a welcoming space for respectful conversation by aspiring to the following ideals:

- Listen well, providing each person with a welcoming space to express her perspective on the issue at hand
- Seek to empathetically understand the reasons another person has for her perspective
- Express your perspective, and your reasons for holding that perspective, with commitment and conviction, but with a non-coercive style that invites conversation with a person who disagrees with you
- In your conversation with a person who disagrees with you, explore whether you can find some common ground that can further the conversation. But, if you cannot find common ground and decide that "we can only agree to

disagree," do so in a way that demonstrates respect for the other and concern for her well-being and does not foreclose the possibility of future conversations.

- In aspiring to these ideals for conversation, also aspire to be characterized by humility, courage, patience, and love

Guidelines for Posting Comments

All comments submitted for the APC eCircle will be read, and the moderator (Harold Heie) will post those comments judged to satisfy the following guidelines.

On the positive side, a good comment has the following qualities:

- specifically relevant to the issue or questions raised by the original post
- reasonably short and concise
- respectful in tone and language (even if you are commenting on something with which you disagree strongly)
- contributes something positive and new to the topic

On the flip side, there are some things you will definitely want to avoid in your comments:

- contributes little that is positive or new to the topic
- overly long or otherwise difficult to read (if your comment is longer than the original post, consider shortening it for readability)
- disrespectful in tone or language (e.g., resorting to name-calling, demonizing a person with whom you disagree, or impugning motives)
- dominating the conversation (although some give-and-take is called for in a good conversation, avoid repeated postings that add little to what you have already said)

Contributors

Amy E. Black is associate professor of political science and chair of the department of politics and international relations at Wheaton College (Illinois). Prior to joining the Wheaton faculty in 2001, she taught at Franklin and Marshall College in Lancaster, Pennsylvania. She is a graduate of Claremont McKenna College and earned her PhD in political science at Massachusetts Institute of Technology. A specialist in American government, her research interests include religion and politics and Congress. She joined Wheaton's faculty after serving as an American Political Science Association Congressional Fellow in the office of Representative Melissa A. Hart (R-PA). Her time in DC gave her the opportunity to apply her academic training and research to the real-world setting of the House of Representatives. She helped write two pieces of legislation (one of which became law), directed the Congresswoman's efforts on education and women's issues, and served as the office's liaison with pro-life and evangelical groups on Capitol Hill. She is the author of several books, including *Honoring God in Red or Blue: Approaching Politics with Humility, Grace, and Reason* (Moody, 2012); *Religion and American Politics: Classic and Contemporary Perspectives*, edited with Douglas Koopman and Larycia Hawkins (Pearson Longman, 2011); *Beyond Left and Right: Helping Christians Make Sense of American Politics*

(Baker Books, 2008); *From Inspiration to Legislation: How an Idea Becomes a Law* (Prentice Hall, 2007); and, with Douglas Koopman and David Ryden, *Of Little Faith: The Politics of George W. Bush's Faith Based Initiatives* (Georgetown, 2004). She regularly contributes commentary to the *Christian Science Monitor* and to the Center for Public Justice's *Capital Commentary*. She and her husband, Wheaton theology professor Dan Treier, live in Wheaton with their daughter. She loves spectator sports, including playing fantasy football each fall and cheering for the Chicago White Sox.

Paul Brink is an associate professor of political science and moderator of the Division of Social and Behavioral Sciences at Gordon College in Wenham, Massachusetts. A Canadian by birth, Paul earned his BA in political science at Redeemer University College (Ontario); MA at Dalhousie University (Nova Scotia); and his PhD at the University of Notre Dame. Prior to arriving at Gordon in 2006, Paul taught at Eastern University, in St. Davids, Pennsylvania. A political theorist by training, Paul also maintains teaching and research interests in comparative politics, focusing in particular on the politics of divided societies. Questions of unity amid diversity also sustain his theoretical interests, focusing on liberal attempts to respond to the challenges of pluralism, and, more broadly, exploring and developing responses to pluralism that are found within the various traditions of Christian political thought. His recent Zylstra lectures, delivered at his alma mater, Redeemer University College, in fall 2012, represent some of his most recent reflections on these subjects. An interest he has only barely begun to consider concerns the new potential for Christian political reflection in the developing world; his article "Negotiating a Plural Politics: South Africa's Constitutional Court" represents an initial exploration of that theme. Paul lives with his wife, Jennifer, and their three children, Jesse, Erin, and Annika, in historic Ipswich, Massachusetts.

David P. Gushee is the Distinguished University Professor of Christian ethics and director of the Center for Theology and Public Life at Mercer University, where he teaches at McAfee School of Theology and throughout Mercer University in his specialty, Christian ethics. He earned his BA at the College of William and Mary (1984), MDiv at Southern Baptist Theological Seminary (1987), and both the master of philosophy (1990) and PhD (1993) in Christian ethics at Union Theological Seminary in New York. As director of the Center for Theology and Public Life, he organizes events and courses to advance quality conversations about major issues arising at the intersection of theology, ethics, and public policy. Beyond his work at Mercer, he is a columnist for the *Huffington Post* and a contributing editor for *Christianity Today*. He has published fifteen books, with four more in development, and many hundreds of essays, book chapters, articles, reviews, and opinion pieces. Probably his most widely noted books are *Righteous Gentiles of the Holocaust* (Fortress, 1994/Paragon House, 2003); *Kingdom Ethics* (IVP, 2003); *The Future of Faith in American Politics* (Baylor, 2008); and a devotional work with his wife, Jeanie, called *Yours Is the Day, Lord, Yours Is the Night* (Thomas Nelson, 2012). His new work, the broadly endorsed *Sacredness of Human Life* (Eerdmans, 2013), interrogates what it has meant, and proposes what it should mean, to say that human life is sacred. He and his wife and their regal cat Noah reside in Atlanta, Georgia, where they eagerly await visits from their grown children Holly (with her husband, Jonathan), David, and Marie. They attend First Baptist Church in Decatur, where he teaches a weekly Sunday School class when in town. David is a long-time Atlanta Braves fan and, at age fifty, still very much enjoys competing with his students and colleagues on the tennis court.

Lisa Sharon Harper, Sojourners' director of mobilizing, was the founding executive director of New York Faith & Justice—an organization at the hub of a new ecumenical movement to end poverty in New York City. In that capacity, she helped establish Faith Leaders for Environmental Justice, organized faith leaders to speak out for immigration reform, and organized the South Bronx Conversations for Change, a dialogue-to-change project between police and the community. She has written extensively on tax reform, comprehensive immigration reform, health-care reform, poverty, racial justice, and transformational civic engagement for publications and blogs including *The National Civic Review, God's Politics* blog, *The Huffington Post, Relevant Magazine, Patheos.com, Urban Faith,* and *Prism*. Having earned her master's degree in human rights from Columbia University, she has written two books that explore the intersection of Christian faith and politics: *Evangelical Does Not Equal Republican or Democrat* (New Press, 2008); and *Left, Right & Christ: Evangelical Faith in Politics* (Russell Media, 2011), which was coauthored with D. C. Innes (an evangelical Republican who is also a member of the Tea Party). She was the recipient of Sojourners' inaugural Organizers Award and the Harlem "Sisters of Wisdom" Award. She was celebrated on Rick Warren's website, purposedriven.com, as one of the inaugural "Take Action Heroes"; was named fifth among the "13 Religious Women to Watch in 2012" by the Center for American Progress; and was recently awarded the 2013 Faith and Justice Leadership Award by the National Black Women's Roundtable. She is a member of Metro Hope Church in New York City, an Evangelical Covenant Church.

Stephen (Steve) Monsma is a senior research fellow at the Paul Henry Institute for the Study of Christianity and Politics, Calvin College (Grand Rapids, Michigan) and a professor emeritus of political science at Pepperdine University (Malibu, California). He was also active in Michigan politics for twelve years: for four years as a member of the Michigan House of Representatives, four years as member of the Michigan Senate, and four years as a gubernatorial appointee. He is the author, coauthor, editor, or coeditor of seventeen books and has published most widely in the fields of public policy, church-state relations, and faith-based nonprofit organizations. His most recent work is an Apple iBook entitled, *Healing for a Broken World: Christian Perspectives on Public Policy.* Among his other recent works are *Pluralism and Freedom: Faith-Based Organizations in a Democratic Society* (Rowman & Littlefield, 2012); and, with J. Christopher Soper, a second edition of *The Challenge of Pluralism: Church and State in Five Democracies* (Rowman & Littlefield, 2009). He has also contributed numerous chapters in various books and published articles in such journals as the *Journal of Church and State;* the *Notre Dame Journal of Law, Ethics, and Public Policy;* and *Religion and Politics.* He and his wife of 47 years, Mary, reside in Grand Rapids, Michigan, and have two adult children and four grandchildren. Steve's chief forms of recreation are reading murder mysteries (he vows to write one himself one day) and spending time and working on his and Mary's Lake Michigan cottage.

Eric Teetsel is executive director of the Manhattan Declaration, a "call of Christian conscience" on life, marriage, and religious liberty founded by Charles W. Colson in 2009 and signed by hundreds of prominent Catholic, Orthodox, and evangelical leaders and more than 500,000 others. The proud son of a career Army officer, he moved numerous times as a child, which led to him spending seven years in the Netherlands, Germany, and Italy. He attended Wheaton College, graduating with a degree in interpersonal communication in 2006. Eric's first career was in higher education administration. After earning a master's degree in college student affairs from Azusa Pacific University, he joined the staff of Colorado Christian University. While at CCU, he served former U.S. Senator Bill Armstrong and was given the opportunity to learn from notable thinkers, including Michael Novak. After two years, the opportunity to construct an innovative program at the American Enterprise Institute presented itself, and Eric moved to Washington, DC. The Values & Capitalism project is aimed at educating evangelical college students about the moral and material nature of the free enterprise system. While at AEI, Eric worked with many of the leading figures in Christian thought, including Jay Richards, Michael Gerson, James Davison Hunter, and Marvin Olasky. After three years, a new opportunity presented itself with the Manhattan Declaration, with Chuck Colson offering Eric the position of executive director just three weeks before he died. Eric is responsible for ensuring that the movement continues to inform the public debate over life, marriage, and religious freedom, and serves the broader coalition of organizations working on these fundamental issues. In 2011, he married Abby, a high school math teacher in Southeast DC. Together with their dog, the couple lives on Capitol Hill, where they can often be found eating frozen yogurt and rooting for the Nationals.

Author

Harold Heie is a senior fellow at The Colossian Forum and at the Center for Faith and Inquiry at Gordon College and served as the founding director of the Center for Christian Studies at Gordon from 1994 to 2003. He previously served as vice president for academic affairs at Messiah College (1988–1993) and Northwestern College in Iowa (1980–1988). Prior to that, he taught mathematics at Gordon College (1975–1980) and The King's College (1963–1975). He has a BME degree from the Polytechnic Institute of Brooklyn (now the Polytechnic Institute of NYU—1957), an MSME from the University of Southern California (1959), and an MA and PhD in mechanical and aerospace engineering from Princeton University (1961, 1965). Harold has held a number of leadership positions at the Council for Christian Colleges and Universities (CCCU), primarily focusing on leading national and regional faculty development workshops. He has spoken or consulted at more than fifty CCCU institutions and now serves the CCCU as a senior fellow. He is also a member of the board of fellows for the PhD program in organizational leadership at Eastern University and has been active for many years with the Center for Public Justice, including serving as a trustee for nine years. His publications include *Soul Care: Christian Faith and Academic Administration* (co-edited with Mark Sargent, Abilene Christian

University Press, 2012); *Mutual Treasure: Seeking Better Ways for Christians and Culture to Converse* (co-edited with Michael King, Cascadia, 2009); *Learning to Listen, Ready to Talk: A Pilgrimage Toward Peacemaking* (iUniverse, 2007); *The Role of Religion in Politics and Society* (co-edited with A. James Rudin and Marvin R. Wilson, Center for Christian Studies of Gordon College & the Interreligious Affairs Department of the American Jewish Committee, 1998); *Slogans or Distinctives: Reforming Christian Higher Education* (co-authored with David Wolfe, University Press of America, 1993); and *The Reality of Christian Learning: Strategies for Faith-Learning Integration* (co-edited with David Wolfe, Eerdmans, 1988). He is an avid baseball fan, cheering for the St. Louis Cardinals since his boyhood days in Brooklyn (even when the LA Dodgers called Brooklyn their home); Stan "The Man" Musial was his boyhood hero.

Contact Information
203 St. Paul Ave. NE
Orange City, IA 51041
(712) 737–8676
hheie@orangecitycomm.net
www.respectfulconversation.net

Acknowledgments

I first want to thank my six regular APC contributors: Amy Black, Paul Brink, David Gushee, Lisa Sharon Harper, Steve Monsma, and Eric Teetsel (with an added word of thanks for Steve Monsma for his very helpful input as I shaped and refined this APC project). Despite their own very busy schedules, these contributors faithfully posted their position papers every three weeks over a period of nine months. I personally benefitted a great deal from my reading of their thoughtful and insightful papers. They are the ones who made this project work.

I also want to thank the readers of our APC who submitted very thoughtful comments on the postings of our six contributors. Your respectful comments added richness to our conversation.

A special word of thanks goes to the leaders at the three organizations that graciously cosponsored this project: Tal Howard, director of the Center for Faith & Inquiry (formerly the Center for Christian Studies) at Gordon College; Kevin den Dulk, executive director of the Henry Institute for the Study of Christianity and Politics at Calvin College; and Stephanie Summers, chief executive officer of the Center for Public Justice.

I also express my thanks to Christina Wassell, who did splendid work in setting up my website, and who served with distinction as my "web manager" throughout this APC project. Her support and encouragement are greatly appreciated.

Finally, I express my deep appreciation to Jim Skillen, to whom I have dedicated this book. Jim and I both arrived at Gordon College in the fall of 1975 to teach political studies and mathematics, respectively. At that point in my life, I was totally apolitical since I had a very narrow view of God's redemptive purposes that limited what God was doing in our world to the salvation of individual people. Through a series of conversations, Jim awoke me from my political stupor, helping me to see that Christians are called to partner with God toward redeeming all of God's creation, including the realm of politics (Col. 1:20).

It was Jim who introduced me to the work of the Center for Public Justice (CPJ), which he founded and served as president for over thirty years. For nine of those years, I had the privilege of serving with Jim on the CPJ Board of Trustees. And in all my encounters with Jim over these many years, he has always exemplified a gracious spirit and has modeled giving others the gift of respectful conversation.

CPSIA information can be obtained at www.ICGtesting.com
Printed in the USA
LVOW06s0920250214

375081LV00004B/5/P